THE BRUMBACK LIBRARY
OF VAN WERT COUNTY
VAN WERT, OHIO

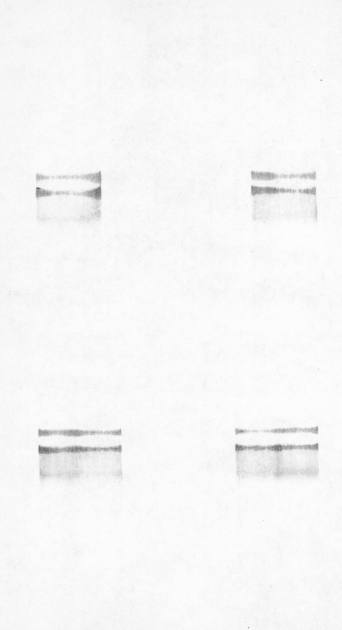

FRONTIER NURSE
Mary Breckinridge

Born: February 16, 1881
Died: May 16, 1965

Mary Breckinridge, a Southern belle, born to comfort and pleasure, chose to dedicate her life to a fight against the tragic infant mortality that blighted the lives of the mountain people of Kentucky. Her dream was to create a nursing service that would reach families who never had known the benefits of medicine. With her staff she rode horseback to the most remote cabins and worked under the most primitive conditions. She died at the age of 84, but the Frontier Nursing Service lives on and with it the memory of an indomitable woman who overcame all odds to turn a humanitarian dream into reality.

Other Books By Katharine E. Wilkie and
  Elizabeth R. Moseley

Father of the Constitution
  James Madison

Teacher of the Blind
  Samuel Gridley Howe

Books By Katharine E. Wilkie

John Sevier: Son of Tennessee

The Man Who Wouldn't Give Up
  Henry Clay

FRONTIER NURSE
Mary Breckinridge

by
Katharine E. Wilkie
and
Elizabeth R. Moseley

JULIAN MESSNER   NEW YORK

SP   RK CD MK LF CADCC

Published simultaneously in the United States and Canada by
Julian Messner, a division of Simon & Schuster, Inc.,
1 West 39 Street, New York, N.Y. 10018. All rights reserved.

**To the Members of the Staff of
the Frontier Nursing Service at Wendover**

Printed in the United States of America
SBN 671-32107-2 Cloth trade
     671-32108-0 MCE
Library of Congress Catalog Card No. 69-13047

Acknowledgments

The authors wish to acknowledge with grateful thanks the assistance given them by Miss Helen E. Browne, Director of the Frontier Nursing Service, Miss Agnes Lewis, Miss Betty Lester, and Miss Lucile Hodges, all members of the Frontier Nursing Service staff at Wendover on the Middle Fork of the Kentucky River.

Mrs. Breckinridge's niece, Mrs. John Marshall Prewitt, her sister, Mrs. Warren Dunn, and her sister-in-law, Mrs. James Crason Breckinridge, were most gracious in replying by letter to queries written them about the founder of the Frontier Nursing Service.

This little book goes into the world as a tribute to a Great Lady—Mrs. Mary Breckinridge.

CONTENTS

CONTENTS

"These Are My Golden Days"

Everything was laughter and gaiety in the old rambling stone house at Hazelwood. Standing high on the ridge above the Harlem River near New York City, this was the home of Mrs. James Lees. Although it was February and there were still open fires in every room, there was a suggestion of spring outside, where a winter sun shone brightly over meadows that rolled down to the water.

Seventeen-year-old Mary Breckinridge, recently returned with the other members of her family from Europe, where her father had been the American minister to Russia during President Cleveland's second administration, accompanied her grandmother as the latter went on her rounds of supervision in the long, low-raftered kitchen. There the two cooks were preparing for the expected guests who would soon begin arriving for the wedding of Susanna Lees, the daughter of the house, and her fiancé, Henry Randolph Sutphen.

Mary watched Mrs. Lees as she inspected the servants at their work. The huge turkeys trussed up and resting in large roasting pans were ready for the oven. Several hickory-smoked hams from Kentucky were already baked and marked into diamond-shaped squares. Fruit pies of several kinds were cooling in the large pie safe. As Mary watched, one of the cooks removed a feathery angel cake from the oven, deftly inverted it, and set it to one side to cool.

Although Mary was not aware, Mrs. Lees was watching her closely. She thought that the girl who had recently come home from Russia differed little from the child who had gone away four years ago —quick to anger, quicker to forget, but vivid, alive and fearless every waking hour.

The Breckinridges had been the first to arrive for Susanna's marriage to young Henry Sutphen. All the family—twenty-year-old Carson, seventeen-year-old Mary, fourteen-year-old Lees, and three-year-old Clif, together with their parents—had returned in January, 1898, just in time for their cousin's wedding. Soon all the various family clans would gather, and the old house would be bursting at the seams.

That was the way she liked it, Mary reflected. Years ago, when her real maternal grandmother had died, "Grandmother Lees" had stepped into the breach and taken her dead sister's place. Mary and the other young Breckinridges hardly knew the difference, although she was actually their great-aunt.

Mrs. Lees was also a Kentuckian by birth and Scotch-Irish by ancestry, and her doors were never closed to kith or kin. More than once she had blessed a kind Providence that had supplied her with a wealthy banker husband and a spacious house on these broad acres above the Harlem River near New

York City, for she enjoyed all visitors and especially her "grandchildren."

Now in the kitchen at Hazelwood she was taking a last look around. "I think everything is under control in this department," she told the servants. "We are ready at last."

The cooks looked up. "Yes, ma'am," the older one agreed. "Don't you worry, Mrs. Lees. We have enough food to feed a regiment."

"And a regiment will soon be arriving," her mistress assured her with a twinkle in her eye.

Mary followed her grandmother down the hall to a rear sitting room where Mrs. Lees wrote her letters and did her sewing. A cheerful fire was burning on the hearth.

"Grandmother, do you still help your Kentucky mountain children?" Mary asked.

"Southern mountain children," Mrs. Lees corrected. "However, it does seem as though a great many of them are in Kentucky. Many sons and daughters of the men who fought for the South need help desperately, and I am happy to aid the cause."

The listening girl's eyes took on a faraway look. "As long as I can remember, you have been helping unfortunate Southern children."

"What better way could I spend my money and my effort?" her grandmother asked quietly. "Reconstruction days after the War Between the States were cruel ones, Mary. Believe me, if I can aid needy boys and girls, many of them in the mountains of Kentucky, to secure an education, I shall have done my bit to place the South once more on a firm and lasting footing."

"You have done much more than help boys and girls you have never seen," Mary told her with warmth. "You have made Hazelwood seem like home to all us Breckinridges. As you know, we have never owned a home of our own. All the years we were in Washington we lived on rented property. Father can never forget that the Federal government confiscated his father's house when he left the Union and joined the Confederacy. While we were in Europe, I was often very lonely, especially in St. Petersburg, but I would think about America and this beautiful home with you in it—and then I wasn't lonely any more."

"Of course not," Mrs. Lees agreed. "That was as it should have been. My doors were open to your mother when she came here as a twelve-year-old girl with my widowed sister. That little girl grew up and married. After my sister died, I became your grandmother, at least in name. Ever since that time you children have made me very happy whenever you spent your summers here."

Mary gave a little laugh. "Sometimes I think my life up till now has been like a shifting kaleidoscope. Mississippi—Arkansas—Washington—Canada—England—Russia—Switzerland—the French Riviera—and now back here again. We always seem to come back to Hazelwood."

"And I hope you always will," Mrs. Lees replied.

"So long as your father is in the diplomatic service, the government is likely to send him any place on the globe. Under those circumstances it is practically impossible for him to establish a permanent home. But we must face conditions as we find them, not as we wish they were. As soon as we get Susanna married to her young man, we must decide what to do with you and Carson. Lees and Clif are still too young for us to be concerned over, but Carson is already a young man, and you are fast on the way to becoming a young lady."

When February, 1898, was over, the wedding of Susanna Preston Lees and Henry Randolph Sutphen was over, too. For days Hazelwood had been the center of so many activities that it seemed one continual house party. To Mary the presence of numerous relatives, the coming and going of many guests, the arrival of multitudinous gifts and the gay talk and banter that pervaded the tapestry of the hours like brilliant-colored threads, provided a make-believe atmosphere that seemed almost unreal.

In a sense, the continent of Europe still seemed her world. She had just returned from four years there, spent for the most part in Russia and Switzerland, with brief interludes in London and Dresden. Her life had been centered against a foreign background. Even now she still felt herself a part of the time when her father, minister at the court of the czars, along with her mother, had been involved in affairs that took them both away from their children.

Mary had spent innumerable dull hours in the very dull company of her French and German governesses, for Lees, three years younger than she, could hardly be considered a companion for her teenage sister. To be sure, Mary adored her brother Carson, but he considered himself too adult to spend much time with his sisters.

If it had not been for books, with which the house was overrun, and her journal, to which she confided her inmost thoughts, her solitary existence would have been unbearable indeed. As it was, the hours at the legation passed slowly, while the great clock in the entrance hall solemnly ticked away the seconds. Once the monotony was broken by the arrival of a new baby brother. Then there were a few other red-letter days as when she attended the coronation of Emperor Nicholas II and Empress Alexandra, but usually one dull day followed another with the national customs of tea drinking in the summer and ice-skating in the winter. She was happy when at last her parents decided to enroll her at the Rosemont-Dezaley School in Lausanne, Switzerland.

There she made friends with Evelyn Hill and two other young Americans, Edith Richie and Nadine Nutall. After that the weeks and months passed all too quickly. The girls lived under a strict but not unpleasant regime, speaking French daily and their mother tongues only on Sunday. Since they came from Germany, Holland and South America, as well as from England and the United States, the weekly day of rest resulted in a mild polyglot confusion.

At intervals the school mistresses took the girls to Lake Geneva, Chillon and other places of interest. No one enjoyed these excursions more than Mary, who had sadly missed the companionship of her peers during the Russian period.

When her school days in Switzerland came to an end, she left the school with mixed emotions, but her sorrow soon came to an end when she joined her family in Dresden for the Christmas season. After a few weeks there, spent mainly in art galleries and at the opera, the Breckinridges booked passage for America and home.

Finally the last detachment of guests and visiting relatives left Hazelwood in a flurry of good-byes. To-morrow Clifton Breckinridge's family, too, would be on their way. Mother, with the two younger children, would go to Oasis, her brother Joe's plantation in the delta region of Mississippi; Father would join them there after he made a short business trip to Arkansas.

"I think you and Clifton have decided wisely," Mrs. Lees said to Mary's mother. "Mary should do well at Miss Low's School in Stamford, and Carson will like the University of Tennessee. Perhaps Mary will want to go to college somewhere after she has finished at Miss Low's School."

Mrs. Breckinridge shook her head. "I hardly think so. In her father's opinion and mine, higher education is a bad thing for women. A woman's place is in the home."

Listening, Mary felt confused. She was not at all certain she wanted more education, yet she viewed marriage with little enthusiasm. She had ambitions which she had as yet confided to no one. Her most eager desire was to travel to the ends of the earth, to seek out the little-known spots in the world, to explore where few human beings had ever set foot. Perhaps the mountain climbing she had experienced when she was in school in Switzerland was responsible for her yearning. There she had known wonder and grandeur—and a sense of achievement. At any rate, the lure of the unknown constantly beckoned to her. In comparison, staying at home and keeping house seemed a mundane business.

With a sinking heart, as she listened to her mother's words, she realized that for a girl at the turn of the century her goal was as remote as the mountains of the moon. Nevertheless, no law forbade her to think about it. And meantime there was the plantation in Mississippi to which she could look forward. At Oasis, with its primeval forests and trackless swamps, she had acquired at an early age a sense of almost limitless freedom. After a few months at Miss Low's School, she would be free to travel to the old home where Uncle Joe Carson and his family would be waiting to welcome her. She had not seen Oasis for five years. For her, returning there would be as great an event as landing on American soil had been after her years in Europe.

The months at Miss Low's passed quickly. As soon as they were over, Mary left immediately for

Mississippi. She felt a warming sense of satisfaction, although she had been happy at the New England school where she had been challenged and intellectually stimulated. During that time in a letter to her mother she had written: "Serious study is a delightful thing."

From the moment she disembarked from the steamboat at Friar's Point and rode seven miles through the pine forest to Oasis, she found that the region and the house equalled and even surpassed her childhood memories. Life was gracious at Oasis with its great old rooms filled with a shadowy past. From the drawing-room walls, the likenesses of her Carson ancestors looked down at her.

She knew that when she visited her father's people near Lexington, Kentucky, the portraits on the walls would be those of Breckinridges with the figure of Grandfather John Cabell Breckinridge always present. He had been Vice-President of the United States under President Buchanan and later Secretary of War in the Confederacy under Jefferson Davis. In the homes of some of the family there were portraits of the Reverend Robert J. Breckinridge and his two sons, one a strong Union man like his father and the other a soldier of the South. Breckinridges always had the courage of their convictions, and the Breckinridge clan was proud of its forebears even when the various members disagreed on national politics. Loyalty to the clan was a way of life to which Mary Breckinridge had been born.

Adventure was as vital to her as the air she

breathed, and there was no lack of adventure at Oasis. In a short time her Uncle Joe and his doctor son by a former marriage found that their young kinswoman had the steady hand and the keen eye of a first-rate hunter. After that discovery she often accompanied them on their hunting trips.

Mary enjoyed deer hunting most of all. It was rough going, even for the men, but she never faltered. Along with her companions she pushed her way on horseback through the tall canebrakes. Brambles and briers slashed at her face, but she hardly noticed them. All this time she carried her rifle on the saddle bow, ready to fire at a moment's notice.

At last to the admiration of her companions, she shot a deer. She received their acclamations graciously, but gave no sign of any emotion. After returning home, she retired to her room, bathed and appeared for the evening meal, looking very much the sheltered young Southern lady. She gave no sign that while one part of her nature felt a fierce pride in her superior marksmanship, the other cringed with feminine horror at the thought of the animal she had killed. From that crucial moment in the canebrakes, she never again raised her rifle to shoot a deer.

Turkey shooting she found more to her liking. She and her companions often rode at daybreak to a spot in the swamps where they could tether their horses. Then, proceeding on foot, they took their stand and waited. They had practiced turkey calling at the plantation house many times. Now they put the skill to a practical use.

One day Mary exercised that skill by calling up a great gobbler to a range of about sixty yards. He was a wary bird and would come no closer, although she used all her arts of imitation. The young man at her side grinned from ear to ear. He was a neighboring plantation owner who wrote for the magazine *Field and Stream* under the pen name of Tripod. Exasperated by his thoroughly masculine attitude, Mary snatched up her rifle, aimed it and fired. The shot rang out. The huge bird quivered for a moment, then fell over and lay still. A look of startled disbelief spread over Tripod's features. "By Jove!" he exclaimed in admiration. "You *are* a shot, Miss Mary."

The real test of her nerve came when she was visiting friends in Memphis. Tripod had heard her express a desire for a hunting belt made of rattlesnake skin. Early one morning, having come up the Mississippi by boat, he arrived with a dray in tow. The drayman carefully lifted down a large box, placed it on the ground and drove away. With her host, his wife and two other visitors, Mary waited expectantly on the verandah.

Tripod's eyes gleamed with mischief as he tossed the horse's reins to a stable boy, picked up the box and lugged it up the front steps. "Here's your belt, Miss Mary," he announced. "But let's have some fun first. Do you remember reading in a recent issue of *Field and Stream* about some lost hunters who kept themselves from starving by killing and eating rattle-snakes? Are you game?"

Mary swallowed hard. "I'm game," she announced.

All five onlookers, among them a girl from Tennessee and a young Englishman visiting America for the first time, waited at a respectful distance as Tripod opened the box. Mary's blue eyes grew larger and the other girl shrieked wildly as an enormous reptile glided out and slithered down the broad steps of the verandah.

"Six feet long, if he's an inch!" Mary cried.

"Head him off!" shouted Tripod.

They ran to obey his command, although the Tennessee girl was decidedly in the rear. Tripod swung a lasso about his head and threw the rope just as the snake coiled. The rattler struggled violently in his trap. Mary held the lasso in both hands as Tripod sprang forward with a forked stick to hold the snake down. Together the pair slipped a cornucopia stuffed with chloroform-soaked cotton over the wicked-looking head. For a few moments the snake thrashed about, and then lay still.

"Whew!" Tripod breathed. "He was a tough specimen. I'll take him to the taxidermist, and you shall soon have your belt."

The next morning he arrived again while the party was waiting on the front verandah to be called to breakfast. This time he bore a small covered dish in one hand and a mischievous smile on his handsome face.

"Rattlesnake meat," he announced. "I had it cooked at a little restaurant where they do that sort of thing rather well."

With these words he made his way toward the kitchen. The girl from Tennessee turned pale and announced in a faint voice that she never had anything but coffee for breakfast. If Mary felt any qualms, she gave no sign. When Tripod reappeared, breakfast was announced.

When they were seated about the long table in the dining room, the cook with the exasperated air of one accustomed by experience to the vagaries of young gentlemen appeared, set the exotic dish squarely in front of Tripod and with her turbaned head in the air departed for the kitchen.

Mary, Tripod and the Englishman sampled the contents of the dish with gusto while their host and hostess ate their usual breakfast. The other girl, looking slightly green, sipped her coffee.

"M-m-m!" Mary pronounced with a waggish air. "It tastes something like 'possum."

2 Preparation for Life

One more year at Miss Low's School ended Mary Breckinridge's school days, but her young womanhood had hardly begun. For the most part that period would be spent at Oasis, Memphis, Knoxville or Hazelwood. An added attraction of the estate on the Harlem River lay in its nearness to the Navy Yard in Philadelphia, where Carson was stationed with the United States Marines. He had left the University of Tennessee at the outbreak of the Spanish-American War, and at its conclusion had decided to make the Marines a lifetime career. Lees, who was now in boarding school, would be sent to Europe later to finish her education.

There were to be times when Mary and Lees would join their parents in the Indian Territory (part of Oklahoma today), where their father, recently appointed by President McKinley, was a member of the Commission to the Five Civilized Tribes. His headquarters were at old Fort Gibson. To the eager Breckinridge girls an absorbing feature of the locality was the presence of dashing Eighth Cavalry troops, replete with daily drill and sound of bugle.

Mary and Lees had their own horses and frequently rode out with their father when he had business on the reservation. The keen-eyed elder daughter observed the many ways in which this minority people was mishandled by the government. At the same time she noticed her father's care and solicitude for them.

Shortly after the turn of the century, Mary and her mother were visiting at Oasis when a telegram informed them of the death of Grandmother Lees. Mary was stunned. It was her first real experience with death, and she could hardly believe that the adored old lady was gone.

On the long journey by train to New York State Mary kept feeling that it could only be a bad dream. But when her grandmother's coachman met them with the carriage at the little Hazelwood station, he wore black livery instead of the usual cream-colored uniform. It was then that Mary met the truth of her loss face to face.

"I shall miss her gentleness, her warmth, her graciousness," she sobbed to her mother. "But do you know what I shall miss most of all?"

"No, dear," Mrs. Breckinridge said. "What shall you miss?"

Mary bit her lips to keep back the tears. "She could always laugh, even at herself. Grandmother could always laugh."

For several summers before Grandmother Lees's death, Mrs. Breckinridge had taken small Clif, who was not a sturdy child, to a boarding house in Canada. Mary had also spent these summers with her mother and little brother on The Brackens, two islands in the Muskoka Lakes. Later when Grandmother Lees died, Mrs. Breckinridge bought these islands with a part of her inheritance. There she built a house, and immediately The Brackens became a center for Carson and Breckinridge kin and especially for the friends of all the younger members of the family.

Mary loved visitors of all ages. She delighted in active sports such as swimming, canoeing and camping. She loved to listen to her elders as they sat around on lazy summer afternoons recounting endless family anecdotes. But there were times when she became tired of it all and longed to get away from everything. Surely there was a purpose in life beyond the gratification of one's own desires, harmless though they were. How was she to find a reason for being—what the French called *une raison d'être?*

The months spent at The Brackens brought no answer to her question. Nor did the time spent in other places. On the surface she lived the carefree life of a typical young Southern girl of her time, circumscribed by the things one could do and the things one could not do. Along with her other female friends, she played at the old old game of courtship without serious intentions.

She learned early to accept compliments and doggerel verse in the same careless spirit young men offered it. She learned that young ladies did not attend any functions that were unchaperoned. She found that one accepted gifts of only books, flowers or candy from male admirers—and always she rode, rode, rode. As far back as she could remember, Mary Breckinridge had been more at home on the back of a horse than off.

It was sometime during these years that she wrote in her journal, which she still kept, a quotation from one of her favorite books: "These are the days of my youth, these are my golden days."

In that same journal she wrote later, after reading Montaigne on friendship:

> Marriage should come only from such an understanding in its most complete and perfect form—for one's husband could not be more than a friend.

And so Mary Breckinridge came to marriage. Of it in her autobiography, *Wide Neighborhoods,* she writes only: "Of my own brief marriage I shall not write except to say that it gave me all, and more than all, I had wanted in married friendship."

In 1906 that marriage ended with the death of her young husband.

The heartbroken young widow was forced to face the dreary outlook of the years ahead. No longer did dreams of exploration call her. Financially she could have followed that path now, but with marriage and the passing of time she had outgrown the desire for it. Neither did she wish to live with her parents, who were enjoying a happy middle age and did not need her. At last she realized that release from her sorrow would come to her only in some form of service.

One day out of sheer boredom, Mary accepted an invitation to visit a girls' school in the mountains of North Carolina where her Grandmother Lees had made several large contributions. While there she offered to sit with a family that had been stricken with typhoid fever. Realizing how much her help was needed and how great were her ignorance and helplessness in the situation, she decided to consult with a family friend, Dr. William Polk of New York City, about the possibility of becoming a nurse.

Before she went on to New York, however, she stopped in Arkansas, where her parents now lived, in order to discuss the matter with them. When she laid her plans before them, they were aghast. In the early years of the twentieth century, young ladies of birth and breeding seldom embarked upon careers. When they did, those careers did not involve disease, suffering, pain, anguish, dirt, germs and the seamy side of life.

"But, my dear girl, this is your home," her father told her anxiously. "There is no need for you to make your own living, especially in nursing. We want you here. Surely you can find opportunities for service in your community, your church—"

His wife laid a restraining hand upon his arm. "Wait, Clif." She turned to their daughter and gave her a searching look. "You are really serious about becoming a nurse, aren't you?"

Mary clasped her hands together tightly. "Oh, yes!"

"Then you must go on to New York. I am sure Will Polk will advise you well." She spoke to her husband, whose face wore a puzzled look. "She *needs* nursing, Clif. She needs it even more than nursing needs her."

In a few days Mary was in New York City where Dr. Polk listened attentively to all she had to say. Then he gave her a letter of introduction to the director of the nursing school at St. Luke's Hospital. Almost before Mary knew what was happening, she was enrolled and ready to start upon her training.

That training was rigorous, especially for probationers who entered the ranks disarmingly innocent of a world where they were expected to be up at dawn and remain on duty for ten hours—which more often than not stretched into eleven, except for night duty, when the hours of service became twelve. In addition to this routine, student nurses were expected to attend classes, listen to lectures by doctors and surgeons and to devote whatever time was left over to study.

Only Mary's innate stubbornness and her will to achieve kept her feet on the path she had chosen. The young widow now had two half-days a week free —welcomed days of rest—and a short annual vacation, which was eagerly anticipated.

Yet the three years of training held much for her besides drudgery. There was so much to learn, so much to do. In spite of the personal grief that at times still swept over her like a flood, she was slowly learning that in service she could find something like a restoration to normal ways of living. The old careless carefree days were gone forever, but in their place was a sense of purpose she had never known before.

Her early days at St. Luke's were a round of sponge baths, bed pans, thermometers and bells. There came the inevitable occasion when a patient under her care died, but death was no stranger to the sensitive young woman who was a little older than the average student nurse. It was now the year 1907, and Mary was twenty-six years old.

As time went on, life in the hospital began to take shape. It was not unusual in those days for a nurse to be called back at night on emergency duty directly after she had gone to the dormitory and fallen exhausted into bed. There was one occasion when Mary met two such calls. There was scarcely time for her to take a bath and get into a fresh uniform before she resumed her usual duties in the operating room. By the time her stint was ended, she had worked for thirty hours without rest or sleep. Clearly St. Luke's was no place for weaklings.

At the end of her second year Mary was sent to the New York Lying-In Hospital which at that time was located in a downtown tenement section of New York. Her closest friend, Willie Biddle, daughter of a Tennessee physician, was assigned to the same place. The two girls found a marked difference in the organization of the two hospitals. At St. Luke's the machinery moved like well-ordered clockwork. In New York Lying-In there was a somewhat casual approach, with each floor a unit in itself. There was little communication between the different areas of the Lying-In Hospital, as both girls were to find out to their sorrow.

Assigned to night duty in one of the nurseries, Mary met with conditions that tore at her heart. The room was crowded with twenty to thirty babies every night. The east wind from across the river seemed to come through the cracks of the old building and permeate the room to its farthest corner. Yet each infant was covered with only one blanket.

Mary's blue eyes flashed as she faced Willie Biddle across a bassinet. "This is ridiculous. This child's legs are actually cold. Something must be done about it."

Nurse Biddle shrugged. "The night supervisor says she requisitioned more blankets weeks ago. What more *can* be done about it?"

Mary was tugging at the sweater she wore over her uniform. "Well, I know what one nurse can do about it."

Her companion hesitated only a minute. Then she followed suit. Two babies at the Lying-In Hospital slept warmer that night.

But not all problems were so easily solved. While most babies were sent to their tenement homes along with their mothers in a matter of days, there were exceptions. One was a pathetic child with a malformed spine.

Mary felt a strange attraction to the patient little creature with the shining brown eyes that seemed to follow her around the room whenever she was in the nursery. Young as Baby Margaret was, the infant seemed to possess the wisdom and understanding of an older child, and Mary was quick to sense that fact.

Because the baby had been there for some weeks, she was bottle-fed after her mother left the hospital. Mary willingly took upon herself the task of preparing the formula and bringing the bottle to the child at scheduled hours.

Standing by the bassinet one night, she spoke thoughtfully to Willie Biddle, who was busy with one of her charges. "I suppose Margaret's mother will soon be taking her away."

Since Willie's mouth was full of safety pins, her reply was not too distinct. Mary could not believe what her ears were hearing.

"What did you say?"

Willie straightened up, removed the offending pins, and spoke loudly and clearly. "Her mother doesn't want her. The night superintendent told me so."

Mary swept her with a look that almost made the other girl draw back. She was glad she was not the object of the white-hot fury that blazed from her friend's blue eyes. Without a word Mary turned on her heel and started for the nursery door.

"Hey, where are you going?" Willie demanded.

Mary flung a reply back over her shoulder. "To find someone with a heart in this hospital—if I can."

Several days had passed when Mary approached Willie one morning in the nurses' dining room. Her eyes were shining.

"You've been up to something," Willie said. "I can always tell."

"Yes—no—well, maybe," Mary confessed. "You see, it's this way. You know, of course, I've been transferred to the Out Patient Department."

Her friend nodded. "I heard it."

"I wish they had postponed it for a little while, but they didn't consult me. Of course I am eager to become a visiting nurse, but at the present moment it interferes with my plans. You've got to help me."

"Me? How?"

Mary drew a deep breath. "I am taking Baby Margaret to rear as my own."

Willie gave a startled gasp, but Mary only nodded in confirmation.

"I am the only person in the world who really wants her. Her mother was relieved to give her up." There was a note of pained disbelief in Mary's voice. "I didn't know that a mother could want to get rid of her baby, but this woman apparently did. I hope her consent constitutes authority."

"But the expense—the responsibility—" Willie faltered.

Mary went on. "Some day when my mother dies and I inherit my share of Grandmother Lees' estate, I shall be what most people would call a rich woman. And I'm not exactly poor at present. I intend to pay Margaret's way in the infants' ward. I want her to learn as she grows older that she is important to someone."

"But, Mary, she probably won't grow older," Willie reminded her. "A baby with an open spine seldom lives to be very old. Such a child can take a turn for the worse very quickly."

Mary silenced her with a look. "It's all settled," she said firmly. "A staff physician has already given me a discharge for her from this hospital. If you will take Margaret to St. Luke's for me when you go off duty this afternoon, I shall breathe more easily. All the arrangements have been made. I won't have any time off until the end of the week, or I wouldn't ask you. Will you do this for me?"

"Of course I will," Willie promised. "And may I add, Mary, you are quite a person."

The matter was not to end so quickly. The next morning before she started on her day's rounds, Mary looked into the nursery. Willie and the baby were gone, and Mary assumed that all was well. She went out on the district and visited her patients in the neighboring tenements in a glow that stayed with her for hours.

It departed abruptly when she reported into the hospital at noon. She was summoned immediately to the head office where she was informed by an irate superintendent that she had been suspended on a charge of stealing a baby. Her friend Willie Biddle had been suspended also, not to mention the cooperating physician.

"But it was all my fault!" Mary cried. "As to stealing a baby, that is perfectly absurd. A staff physician released her. Her own mother does not want her. Miss Biddle merely carried her to St. Luke's for me."

The furore soon died down. Each of the trio was called before a special board to explain matters. In a few hours the suspensions were lifted, but Baby Margaret was brought back to the Lying-In Hospital. It was Mary's first experience with arbitrary red tape, and she found herself unable to cut through it. She was forced to bow to authority. During the remaining months, Mary never allowed a day to pass without visiting Margaret, who seemed to watch for her. Even the other nurses noticed the attachment of the frail mite to her self-appointed protector.

At last Mary finished her duties at the Lying-In Hospital and was transferred back to St. Luke's. She made the change unwillingly, for she did not want to leave Margaret behind. Two days later she received a telephone message that the child had suddenly become worse and died. Being a nurse and knowing about the infant's malady, she was not surprised. Sorrowfully she made arrangements for burial in a neighboring cemetery and went with a kindly minister to watch the tiny casket lowered into the ground.

"Why?" she asked herself, turning away from the small mound of earth. "Why?" The heartbreak of all humanity was in that question.

It was well for Mary that she had returned to St. Luke's. The appalling conditions that existed in the tenement houses which she had visited in her district filled her with horror. At that time many of the two-room flats had only one window which opened on an air shaft. The only light in the second room came from a gas jet. A single toilet on the first floor was used by all the tenants in the large building. The sight of these deplorable features about which she could do nothing depressed her even more than she realized at the time.

In 1910, three years after she entered St. Luke's, Mary stood with the other members of her graduating class and repeated the Florence Nightingale Pledge:

> "I solemnly pledge myself before God, and in the presence of this assembly, to pass my life in purity and to practice my profession faithfully. I will abstain from whatever is deleterious and mischievous, and will not take or knowingly administer any harmful drug. I will do all in my power to maintain and elevate the standard of my profession, and will hold in confidence all personal affairs committed to my keeping and all family affairs coming to my knowledge in the practice of my calling. With loyalty will I endeavor to aid the physician in his work, and devote myself to the welfare of those committed to my care."

When the long training period was over, she went directly to her parents' home in Fort Smith, Arkansas, where her father was now head of a trust company. Except for the summer home at The Brackens, the elder Breckinridges were living in the first home they had ever owned. Mary enjoyed its hospitable spaciousness and above all the abundant shelves for the still-growing library that continued to spill over into every room.

Finding her mother in poor health, she lost no time in taking her to New York and St. Luke's Hospital for a thorough examination. When they left the hospital, it was time to go to The Brackens for the summer. Although Mrs. Breckinridge's health was gradually improving, she gladly turned the housekeeping duties over to her eldest daughter. Sometimes as many as fifteen guests were present on the island. During those summer months Mary discovered that she had a talent for organization.

When the family returned to Fort Smith, Arkansas, in October, Mrs. Breckinridge was ready to resume her place as mistress of the house. Mary was a full-fledged graduate nurse now and no longer needed at home, but still she lingered on.

She seemed to be postponing the day when she would start her nursing career. If her friends wondered why, they learned the reason when she married again, this time a professor in a small Southern college. When their son Breckie (Breckinridge) was born, Mary like all mothers was quite sure he was a wonder child.

While he was still an infant, the guns of August, 1914, exploded upon the world. Indirectly Mary was involved, for her mother and sister, who were traveling in Norway, were caught up in the mad homeward rush of American tourists. Carson became an attaché in Russia before America's entrance into the war. Clif enrolled in officers' training camp, and Lees went to France in service for the YMCA.

Although Mary felt in some degree the war "to make the world safe for democracy," it really scarcely touched her in her sheltered existence as a wife and a mother.

The weeks and the months passed. In 1916, shortly before the birth of a daughter, she engaged a French-Swiss nurse, Juliette Carni, for Breckie who was not yet three.

Mary's daughter Polly was born and lived only a few hours. Her brief sojourn upon this earth served to deepen the friendship between Mary and Juliette —a friendship that would last as long as Juliette lived.

Loved and adored, Breckie grew and thrived. Like any developing youngster, he took on the color of his environment, including a soft Southern accent from his first nurse and then a French one from Juliette.

In January, 1918, a few days after his fourth birthday, tragedy struck. Breckie succumbed to a swift illness and died on January 23. For a time the light of the whole world went out for his mother.

As the succeeding months passed, her marriage broke up, and eventually she was allowed by the court to resume her maiden name. She knew that her years as a wife and a mother were finished.

What the future would hold she did not know, but at the time of Breckie's death she had written in her journal:

> There is a work beside which all other strikes me as puerile—the work which seeks to raise the status of childhood everywhere, so that finally all of the little ones come into the health which is their due.

3 Mary Becomes a Card

After the initial shock of Breckie's death, Mary Breckinridge began once more to submerge her sorrow in a life of service. She decided that northern France, which she already knew and loved, devastated for nearly four years by war, was the place where she could be of the greatest service to children. She planned to go there in June, but found herself barred by a ruling of the State Department that no woman with a brother in the military service could be assigned duty in the war area. Her younger brother Clif was quartered in Germany with the United States Army.

While Mary waited for a change in the ruling, she was not idle. Although she had already enrolled in the American Red Cross Nursing Service, she now obtained permission from the head of that organization to work with the Children's Bureau, under the Child Welfare Department of the Council of National Defense. Her duties were to report on the condition of the nation's children and to make speeches in their behalf wherever she was sent.

At last the regulation about brothers was revoked. As soon as she was notified, the young nurse sped east to make her report to the Children's Bureau and to arrange final preparations for her voyage to France.

Upon arriving in Washington, D. C., she found that city in the throes of the influenza epidemic of 1918. Almost no nurses were available. Immediately Mary volunteered for service. The city was divided into four medical areas, and she was assigned to one of them as assistant to the nurse in charge. During the emergency Mary again worked night and day trying to save the lives of her fellow men.

Thousands of people were in each area, and many of them were stricken with the virulent disease. Conditions were desperate. In Mary's area of about forty thousand patients, there were five nurses. The head nurse soon became ill, and Mary was assigned to replace her. Again she showed her talent for organization by seizing the meager help at hand and utilizing it in the best possible way.

With hundreds of aides, mostly young government employees and elderly physicians, many of whom had not practiced for years, Mary and her untiring nurses saw the emergency through. One thing she discovered. During her house-to-house visits in the nation's capital she found slums worse than any she had seen in New York during her nurse's training days.

By the time the influenza epidemic had spent itself, the Armistice had been signed on November 11, 1918, and the Red Cross no longer wanted nurses for European service. That made no difference to Mary. She knew that children in France needed help, and to France she intended to go.

One afternoon at a tea sponsored for the benefit of

the American Committee for Devastated France, she met its first vice-president, Miss Anne Morgan, daughter of J. P. Morgan of Wall Street. This self-reliant, vigorous, middle-aged woman was the guiding light of CARD (Comité Américain pour les Régions Dévastées de la France). Mary noted that she seemed to know exactly what she was doing and where she was going. Her attitude struck a spark in the heart of the nurse who was fashioned in the same mold.

"Why couldn't I serve in CARD?" she asked.

Miss Morgan gave her a forthright look. "Why not? When would you like to volunteer?"

"Now," Mary answered.

In an unbelievably short time she found herself accepted and on board a ship bound for France.

After a brief interlude in Paris with Lees, who had married a member of the American armed forces and was now Mrs. Warren Dunn, Mary reported for duty at Vic-sur-Aisne, a small town north of Paris. She found her new surroundings in a state of utter devastation. Not only were the tiny hamlets in the area in ruins, but unexploded shells and hand grenades made day-to-day existence a precarious business. The fields were a mass of shell holes, trenches, barbed wire and dugouts. Transportation was at a standstill, for railroads had been destroyed during the war.

Before long one train a day began running from Paris to Vic. All other supplies were brought over the nearly impassable terrain by trucks driven by Frenchmen or volunteer CARD chauffeurs.

Mary was housed with the other members of the unit in a partly shelled old country house on the Aisne. She marveled at the miracle of organization which began to supply the immediate needs of the French population. These were food, clothing, supplies and seeds. CARD supplied these, free at first and later at wholesale prices, as the peasants began to get on their feet once more. Mary noted that this method preserved their pride and innate dignity.

As the program got under way, she asked and received permission from her supervisors to start a special program for war-devastated children, especially those under six, and for pregnant mothers. "This is where I would like to put my time and effort," she explained. "After all, the hope of France lies in its children."

The director smiled at her. There was a strengthening quality about this young middle-aged woman who approached insurmountable tasks with unshaken confidence. Just to be around Mary Breckinridge was to absorb optimism.

"Go ahead," Miss Parsons told her. "I am not sure what you hope to accomplish, or how you hope to accomplish it, but you can do it if anybody can."

In writing home to her mother, Mary described a French peasant family which was existing in a state of slow starvation. They were typical of thousands of other families. Although there were a few milch goats in the countryside, the coveted animals supplied milk to only a handful of fortunate children. Mary looked at the beasts with longing. At the conclusion of her letter to her mother she wrote: "I wish

I had a thousand goats right now. I wish I had fifty."

The weeks passed. Mary never gave another thought to the wish she had flung out in the same spirit one might wish for the moon. Then suddenly letters began to pour in from America. She found that the members of her family were rallying to her cause. So were their friends and acquaintances. Mary placed the checks and drafts in the hands of her chief, Miss Anne Morgan, in Paris and asked her to purchase the goats in carload lots.

One day when she came back to headquarters after making her daily rounds, she heard a sound she could not identify. For a moment she listened outside the dispensary door before she turned the knob and entered. Then she started back in surprise. A large white nanny goat was standing squarely in the middle of a case of nursing bottles. The animal had already knocked over the infant scales and was now chewing contentedly on a dark blue ledger.

"I'm so glad to see you I could hug you!" Mary informed the goat ecstatically.

"You haven't seen anything yet," said a voice behind her.

Mary turned quickly. Two other nurses in uniform stood there, their faces wreathed in smiles.

"There are twenty-eight more goats behind the kitchen," the first girl informed her. "Don't expect much lunch. The cook is out back milking the goats."

"A whole carload arrived from Paris," the other

nurse chimed in. "You should have seen the excitement. We led the triumphal procession from the
freight car. Everyone off duty turned out to bring the
goats to headquarters. All the people in Vic, young
and old, trailed along behind us. It was a beautiful
sight!"

All three were laughing, but Mary's eyes were
moist. All she could see in her mind's eye were the
hollow-eyed, listless children who would soon be
plump and rosy from feeding on goats' milk.

The first carload of goats was soon followed by
others. There was every kind of goat one could
imagine—large, small, medium-sized, gray-black,
white, dappled, brindled. Distributed over the countryside, the goats formed a long step toward the restoration of health to French babies who were emaci-
ated from the lack of proper food.

With the advent of the goats and the coming of
supplies from various agencies that were closing
down with the end of the war, the situation was
greatly improved. When famished mothers were
given large quantities of malted milk, condensed
milk and powdered chocolate, they found themselves
once more able to nurse their babies.

"Things are picking up," Mary said one day in a
grateful voice, "but there's still plenty to do. Thank
goodness there's one thing we aren't responsible
for."

"What's that?" inquired her companion.

"Delivering babies. These French peasant women
have never heard of calling a doctor. The midwives

have apparently been taking care of that since the beginning of time. And they do a magnificent job. All of them seem to be intelligent and well-trained."

Along with the other "Cards," Mary worked long hours under primitive conditions and dropped exhausted at night on a crude pallet, but she realized that the strenuous routine she led had one advantage. She had little time to think of the years that were past, and she felt richly rewarded by the gratitude of the mothers with whom she worked.

The Vic librarian, "Kit" Carson, poked her head in at the door of the dispensary where Mary was working on her reports.

"Mrs. Dike is here and would like to see you."

Mary raised her head in surprise. "The commissioner—all the way from Paris? What could she want?"

"There's only one way to find out," Kit told her, humming a gay little French tune as she went back down the hall.

A little later Mary faced her superior officer in the main office. Mrs. Dike looked with approval at the American woman in her smart-looking uniform of horizon blue with the metal griffons on the lapels. Although Mary was completely unaware of the fact, she presented a very pleasing picture.

"I have been hearing some very nice things about your visiting-nurse service," Mrs. Dike told her.

Mary's face lighted up with pleasure. "There is really nothing to it. I just built on the service already supplied by the Gouttes de Lait, the organization that operated baby milk stations before the war."

"But first you had to reactivate the Gouttes de Lait," Mrs. Dike reminded her, "not to mention the services of the Assistance Publique, which paid for a physician to weigh and examine all babies brought to the town hall."

"They had no follow-up," Mary told her indignantly. "All that work was wasted without a visiting-nurse service. That is why I organized one. The nurses perform a multitude of duties. They see that free milk is supplied in the small towns as well as the large ones. They teach the mothers how to prepare and handle the milk. They have stations throughout the countryside to weigh the babies and train the mothers how to care for them. In short, they render whatever service is needed wherever it is needed."

Mrs. Dike nodded. "That is good. I want you to organize one to cover our sector."

Mary gasped. "Mrs. Dike! That's a large order. I can't do it without fully trained nurses. Where would I get them? We can't spare any more from CARD."

"Why don't you try Dr. Anna Hamilton at the Florence Nightingale School at Bordeaux?" Mrs. Dike asked.

"It all sounds so big!" Mary said weakly.

"I have noticed that you seem to have the ability to get big things done. Don't fail me, Mary."

Mary Breckinridge did not fail her. Writing to Dr. Hamilton, she found the celebrated physician more than agreeable to the idea. In September, 1919, the first nurse arrived from Bordeaux. Mary installed her in the canton of Coucy. The second one she took to the same place. Upon the third she bestowed the county of Vic with the town of the same name. By the end of the year four more nurses from the Florence Nightingale Hospital were placed in villages near Soissons. The visiting-nurse service was now functioning throughout the entire CARD territory.

Before Mary took a leave of absence in March, 1920, she saw the visiting-nurse service established at Soissons. Moreover, CARD was cooperating with the Rockefeller Foundation, which had established a dispensary to treat tuberculosis patients at the Soissons hospital. Mary's responsibilities were growing by leaps and bounds.

After a visit home to America, she returned to France in June of the same year, to realize a little sadly that she could spend less and less time at Vic. Her duties as director of the nursing service carried her into a much broader area that could not be centered in the little town on the Aisne.

About this time she went to Reims to see two women, the director of a Comité Britannique and her associate. Both women were nurses and midwives. The British Committee had been established during the war for direct relief, but now that the funds were giving out, the unit would have to be dissolved.

"It grieves me to leave the little ones," the English director told Mary. "Heaven only knows what will become of them. Their families are living in ruined buildings, huts, any shelter they can find. Our nurses work day and night to keep sickness and epidemics to a minimum, and when we leave—"

Her associate interrupted, "The city fathers have offered us free quarters and free utilities, but these items are only a drop in the bucket. Our operating expenses are tremendous, and there are no more funds. I suppose we must close our doors. It seems inevitable."

Mary did not answer. Her friends were a little surprised, for she was never unresponsive. Then they realized that she was in a deep study. Presently a smile broke over her face.

"Celia, do you think you could prepare an approximate budget for me immediately?" she asked.

"I'll give you a copy of the one I already have," the director told her.

"Good. I'll pack a bag and catch the next train to Paris."

She was off like a streak. The nurses eyed her departing back and then looked at each other.

"Now what do you suppose she is up to?" the first one asked in a surprised tone.

"I don't know," the other said with a chuckle, "But I have high hopes. Mary can pull a rabbit out of a hat, put life into a dead cow—in other words, perform any necessary miracle. We shall just have to wait and see."

Thirty-six hours later Mary Breckinridge returned

from Paris. She wore a triumphant air as she confronted her friends in the office of the Comité Britannique.

"Mission accomplished!" she announced triumphantly. "Everything is arranged. Mrs. Dike has agreed that CARD will take over your Reims unit. Celia, as co-director with me, you will be in complete charge of the Reims nurses. You, Hermione, will also be a co-director. Those precious babies will not lose their chances to become future citizens of France."

That night alone in her room Mary surveyed the situation with a thankful if aching heart. Since time and chance had removed her own children from her, at least she could work to make life easier for other babies and their mothers. In service there was healing.

As the months passed, Mary's friendship with Celia du Sautoy and Hermione Blackwood grew and deepened. In November, 1920, she visited the latter in London, where she had returned for a much needed rest. There, in the city she had visited as a girl, she met through Lady Hermione the leaders of the English nursing world. To Mary it was interesting that all were midwives as well as nurses. The idea was growing in her mind that under many circumstances a nurse must be able to perform both functions. Mary Breckinridge's horizon was extending.

Late that year she wrote her mother that one more year would find her feet permanently upon American soil. She felt that her work in France was drawing to a close. When she broke the news to her superiors, they protested—but her mind was made up. In another year her work would be finished, and well-trained personnel could carry on. While she had not yet decided on a definite plan of service, she knew in her heart that she must return to America. Her people were there. Her roots were there. Her place was there. In other words, Mary Breckinridge was feeling pangs of homesickness.

4 Au Revoir and Bon Jour

When Mary returned to her work in France, there remained in the back of her mind the memory of the many women she had met in London who were both successful nurses and midwives. To her, as an American, the combination was unusual. At that time not even one school for midwives existed in the United States. She shelved the thought of the combination for the time being and went back to her business.

Of this much she was certain: If the Child Hygiene and Visiting Nurse Service, created first by CARD for the Aisne Valley, were to grow and flourish, there must first be available an ever-increasing supply of trained nurses. From her observations in the hospitals of Paris, Mary knew that trained nurses in that city were almost nonexistent.

In a country where successful midwifery had become virtually a science, nursing was a hit-and-miss affair. To her surprise and consternation she discovered that the root of the problem lay in the tremendous political power of the employees who were holding hospital jobs. They did not want to take the stringent training necessary to produce superior nurses. On one occasion in the past, they had threatened to strike when the Assistance Publique attempted to found a modern school of nursing at the great old four thousand-bed hospital of Salpetrière in Paris. Having the bit in their teeth, these hospital employees consented finally to a course of instructions. The modern school of nursing which was proposed had to be given up when the attendants of all the Paris hospitals went on strike. The course of instruction to which they finally agreed was so inferior that even the enrollees who had failed the course were permitted to become attendants of some kind.

Miss Morgan, Mrs. Dike and Mary Breckinridge realized quite well that the visiting-nurse service they had established could not grow without modern schools of nursing in the large hospitals. At Miss Morgan's request Mary undertook a study of the Paris hospitals with a view to presenting a plan to establish a school of nursing in at least one of them. Miss Morgan herself would raise the money for it.

With this purpose in mind Mary became a constant visitor in the Paris hospitals. She walked through ward after ward to talk with the attendants and the patients. She met the great physicians and surgeons of the city, who proved highly cooperative. They suggested that CARD have its school of nursing separate from the hospitals, but take over certain surgical, medical and pediatric wards in them. The idea seemed feasible.

Mary and her committee obtained an interview with a government official. They presented their plan, telling him that CARD would finance a modern school of nursing in certain wards. All they needed was his consent. They did not get it because he feared the political power of the vast army of hospital employees as much as his predecessor had feared it. The door was slammed in the faces of Mary and her co-workers just as it had been slammed years before to the school proposed for the Salpetrière.

Undaunted, Mary hit upon another plan to secure a school of nursing. If Mohammed would not come to the mountain, then the mountain must come to Mohammed. She knew how the French felt about their children. She knew how earnestly they desired to cut down the infant mortality rate. Very well. The public eye must be directed toward the abuse of power by the employees in the public hospitals. She was confident that when that came to pass, the French people would take care of the rest. Someone who knew the facts must prepare to carry the truth across the length and breadth of France.

Miss Morgan and Mrs. Dike agreed heartily with her, but insisted that she was the one to spearhead the movement. Mary shook her head. Her face was turned toward America—but she knew just the woman for the job. CARD had sent a brilliant woman named Marcelle Monod to America on a scholarship to study public health. Mary felt that this talented nurse would fill the post perfectly. She could spread the word among her countrymen about how the bottle-fed babies in the ward were sometimes literally starving to death. As the workers moved from crib to crib with clocklike precision, placing a bottle in each baby's mouth, they often did not take time to see if the milk came out too fast. Sometimes the infants choked on it. Sometimes the bottles fell from their mouths and drained out on the sheets. Mary felt that the public must be made aware of these deplorable conditions. She felt that Madame Monod would command the attention of her fellow citizens more successfully than a foreigner like herself. It was just as well for her peace of mind that she could not foresee that her plans for Madame Monod would never materialize.

Not every moment of Mary's stay in Paris was spent in drudgery and frustration. She had many friends, both English and French. Her cousins, John Breckinridge and his wife Isabella, were there for a few weeks. Mary loved the opera and the theater, and in spite of the profession to which she was dedicated snatched a few hours here and there to refresh her body and revive her spirit.

All her life Mary Breckinridge would prove herself an all-around individual who mixed a healthy amount of recreation with a colossal amount of work. During the winter of 1920, when she was making her exhaustive study of Paris hospitals, she managed a three-week stay with her Breckinridge cousins in the south of France at Cannes. Years before she had spent a Christmas there with her parents, Carson, Lees and little Clif.

Longing to return home, she knew she could not leave until late in the following year. But the days at Cannes did her good, and the load of organizing a school of nursing no longer rested on her shoulders alone. She knew she would soon be placing the matter in Madame Monod's capable hands and was content to let it rest there.

In the summer of 1921, although she was director of twenty-nine nurses, she found it necessary to supervise the entire Aisne area herself. Continually on the move, she recognized the necessity of moving her headquarters to Soissons, although it grieved her to leave her beloved little town of Vic.

As usual she kept constantly busy. A big-hearted group of Swiss citizens offered to keep a large number of French children for an indefinite period. Passports, birth certificates, parental permissions and a variety of other papers were necessary. This was only the beginning of the endeavor, but she saw it safely under way. The Swiss committee of CARD took care of 3,200 children for periods lasting from six months to several years.

The summer of 1921 was one of the hottest on record. There was an epidemic of dysentery in the commune of Blérancourt. Mary's power of endurance was taxed to the utmost. To add to the misery that surrounded her, there was a shortage of serum. In all there were 128 cases with nine deaths, seven of them children. She grieved especially for the children.

Although she had planned to return to America early in September, she delayed her sailing several weeks, at the request of Miss Morgan, in order to accompany the latter on the *Paris*. During the voyage the two would talk over plans for the hospital training school.

But first much remained to be done. Finally Mary tied together the last loose end of business and made a final tour of inspection to see that all was well. The Vic unit gave her a farewell party. The unit at Soissons followed with another. As she listened to the endless speeches and tributes, the suspicion of a smile played around the corners of her mouth. She repeated to herself a haunting line from an old nursery song: "Lawk-a-mercy! Lawk-a-mercy! Can this be I?"

But almost at once her thoughts took a different turn. She had been in France for more than two years. Although this part of her life was ending, she would never forget it. An endless procession of French mothers and babies passed before her mind's eye. She had done her part to restore them to normal living, and now her work in France was done. Across the ocean there was a special mission waiting for her. She did not know what it would be, but with that sixth sense, which all her life was a part of her, she was certain she would recognize it when the proper time came. Meanwhile there was New York and the Statue of Liberty and a loving welcome from her family waiting for her.

Mary's homecoming was saddened by the death of her mother, less than a month after she arrived home. It was a sad reunion when the family gathered for the funeral. Mrs. Breckinridge was buried in the cemetery at Lexington, Kentucky, where Mary's paternal grandfather rested. After the services the family scattered once more. Carson returned to his duties at the Naval War College in Newport, while Lees, who was expecting a baby, returned home and took their father with her. Only Clif, still in the American army in Germany, had been unable to be with them. It fell to Mary's lot to close the houses at Fort Smith and The Brackens.

Not long after the funeral Carson managed to come to Fort Smith for a week to help his sister go through papers that were the accumulation of a lifetime. Mary watched with nostalgic sadness as most of them went into the fire.

"I feel as though you are burning a part of us," she told him.

"You can't carry around stacks of cancelled checks, old receipts and fishing-tackle catalogs the rest of your life," he said. His eyes fell on a collection of articles carefully stacked in a corner of the hall. "We are keeping a part of us, too," he reminded her.

Mary looked fondly at the Sully portrait of their great-great-grandfather John Breckinridge in its classic gold-leaf frame.

"We must put that in fireproof storage along with the other family pieces," she said.

Carson nodded as he continued to sort letters. There was silence in the room for a few minutes. Then Mary spoke.

"You can't put your most important effects in

storage," she announced. "While there are certain things in this house and a few more at The Brackens which I shall never dispose of, they aren't my dearest possessions."

Her brother looked up from his work. He shared a great many ideas with Mary, and he thought he knew what she meant.

"A great deal of money will come to us from Grandmother Lees when Mother's estate is settled," she said slowly, "but money is good only for what it will buy. More than all the money in the world I cherish my childhood memories of Grandmother Lees and Hazelwood. I loved Oasis and Uncle Joe, too. And Mother—there wasn't a time when I haven't known she was deeply interested in every-thing that concerned me."

Carson listened quietly as she went on.

"I don't know what I should have done without her," Mary said. "After I left home for good, she was my pillar of strength, my Rock of Gibraltar, my light in the darkness. I tell you, Carson, intangibles like my memories of Mother—and Breckie—are my most precious possessions."

Carson drew a deep breath. He had been more concerned about Mary than he cared to admit. Wearied by her rehabilitation work abroad, she had returned home only to be faced by her mother's death. The image of his sister's white drawn face with dark circles under her eyes had stayed with him after he had returned east from the funeral. He had found her no different upon his return a few weeks later. However, the one-sided conversation which had just occurred had seemed to bring her some sort of release—and for that he was thankful.

She rose to her feet. "Now I must get busy. There is so much to do before I can leave for Kentucky. I think I told you that I am stopping for a visit with Cousin Molly, Cousin Letitia and Cousin Cabell Breckinridge in Lexington. I'm so glad, Carson, that you and I will be together for a little while at The Brackens this summer. It may be a long time before we see each other again. My plans are made for the next year. I'm not sure where I shall be after that, but this much I know: It will be where I can be of use to children. In that way I shall always feel somehow that I am near Breckie and Polly."

In the early summer of 1922, Mary stopped in the Bluegrass country, as she had planned, on her way to The Brackens. She always looked forward to the warm hospitality of her father's native town. This time, due to her mother's recent death, that hospitality was slightly tempered, but it was present nevertheless.

When her visit was ended, Mary boarded an eastbound train with her mind in a pleasant confusion of swiftly passing days with the Bullocks, the Prestons, the Breckinridges and other relatives. There had been meetings with friends, too. Etched on Mary's memory was the kind, homely face of Linda Neville, who for years had been working tirelessly to remove from mountain people the curse of trachoma, a

dread disease which often caused blindness. Whenever she was present at any gathering, the conversation turned sooner or later to the people of the hills,
their problems, their deprivations and above all their
sterling worth.

As the train sped along, Mary became lost in her
thoughts. They were centered in the mountains of
Kentucky. A long time ago Grandmother Lees had
planted a seed in her mind. That idea had flourished
during her recent years in France. On her visit to
Lexington Linda Neville had brought the idea to full
fruition.

With the welfare of small children always upper-
most in her heart, her friend's word picture of the
deplorable conditions in the hill country had stirred
her to action. To what better use could she now put
her life than to offer it in behalf of tiny babies and
pregnant mothers in a region where doctors were
few, nurses almost unknown and ignorance
abounded?

Staring with unseeing eyes at the landscape outside, she envisioned what the country would be like
if it were served by nurses who went to the patients
in remote localities when the patients could not
come to them. After all, the nursing service in
France had worked that way when conditions made
it necessary. The plan seemed impossible and
yet—

She shook her head to clear it of nebulous impos-
sibilities and rose to go to dinner. A good steak and
a baked potato should change her from a visionary

to a practical-minded person. Yet a small voice within her persisted in telling her that she could combine the roles.

In a few days Mary reached The Brackens and spent the summer there. By the time she was ready to leave, the house on The Brackens had passed into the hands of strangers. Carson bought the smaller island, although he knew he would seldom find the time to return there. When Mary left Canada to enroll at Columbia University in New York, she knew for a certainty what she wanted. Her future would lie in the mountains of Kentucky.

When she arrived in the city, she found living quarters at a small hotel within walking distance of Teachers College. The year proved a good one. With public-health nursing as her main objective, she enrolled in classes in psychology, mental hygiene, social sciences, biology and statistics. As the weeks passed, her plans assumed a definite form. She would spend the coming summer in a survey of an isolated part of the Kentucky mountains—Leslie County, Knott County and Owsley County. After that she would go to England to study midwifery and see midwifery services in operation, for as yet no schools of midwifery existed in the United States. Then and only then would she launch her ambitious project in the mountains of Kentucky.

Wherever Mary Breckinridge went, she soon made friends. While she was in New York, she found herself a frequent visitor in the apartment of Miss Adelaide Nutting, the leader of the nursing depart-

ment of Teachers College at Columbia. Mary found
it satisfying to have this great nurse-teacher approve
her plans relating to the Kentucky mountains.

Evidently Miss Nutting approved of Mary as a
person, too. When the latter visited the older nurse
on Christmas afternoon, her hostess thrust a thin
gift-wrapped package into her hands as she was
leaving.

"I want you to have this," she said abruptly. "I
know of no one who will appreciate it more."

Back in her bedroom when Mary had time to
examine the contents of the package, she found that
it was a small brown volume bearing definite signs of
age and wear. The author was Florence Nightingale.

Another of Mary's friends was Dr. Ella Woodyard, who was doing educational research with the
well-known psychologist, Dr. Edward Lee Thorn-
dyke, at Teachers College. Like others, Dr. Woodyard caught fire from Mary's enthusiasm and was
soon talking about the projected mountain survey as
though it were her own idea.

As summer drew nearer, Mary approached her
with a proposal. "I need your help," she told her. "In
my own mind I am sure a nurse-midwife service in
the mountains is vital, but I must have statistical
facts."

"You intend to spend the summer collecting them,
don't you?" her friend asked.

"About midwives, yes," Mary answered. "I must
see the country and the conditions firsthand. Up till
now I have relied mainly on what others have told

me. But there are some things I can't do. That is where you come in."

Dr. Woodyard did not answer immediately. She had learned it was best to allow Mary to tell her story in her own way.

"People who ought to know tell me that mountain people are fine and intelligent," Mary went on. "They certainly should be, for they are descendants of settlers who first opened up and tamed very rugged country. However, I want to know the facts. This plan of mine for a nursing organization will take a tremendous amount of money. I can't expect to get contributors unless I have evidence showing that the mountain children are worth saving. As a psychologist, will you go with me and give some individual mental tests?"

Ella Woodyard's eyes shone with anticipation. "Try to keep me away! I'll join you the last few weeks in Kentucky and give all the tests you need."

Mary laughed. "We're as good as on the way. This should be a great summer!"

5 From Kentucky to Europe

Mary Breckinridge came to the mountains of Kentucky in the summer of 1923. She was not the first of that name to travel through the Appalachians. In 1793 her great-great-grandfather, John Breckinridge, had brought his wife Mary, better known as Polly, and their two small children across southeastern Pennsylvania, down the Ohio to Limestone (now Maysville), and overland through the wilderness to Lexington, Kentucky, at that time a flourishing frontier town.

Now in the twentieth century another Mary Breckinridge had arrived. She had come to make a survey of midwives in the counties of Leslie, Knott and Owsley, where conditions were especially rugged. Forced to travel on horseback, she was seldom able to find a respectable mount. During the course of the summer she rode thirteen horses and three mules. Saddles were almost unknown in the area. Bridles and girths were usually homemade. As for horseshoes, she always carried a few in her saddlebags, to be certain that her horse stayed shod.

Her father had come for the summer to Boone Tavern in Berea, where he could see his daughter now and then on weekends. She planned to go to England in the fall for her midwifery training, which could not be secured at that time in the United States. Father and daughter snatched at occasional visits together in the picturesque little college town in the foothills, whenever she could spare a short time from her absorbing duties.

The survey of midwives in the area proved a revealing experience. Mary pressed into the hills and the hollows on horseback to interview the midwives, whose business it was to bring the mountain babies into the world, since there were no licensed physicians for hundreds of square miles.

Mary talked with fifty-three midwives that summer. In her mind she classified them as dirty, fairly clean and clean. Although they ranged in age from thirty to ninety years, most of them were ancient wrinkled crones. Among the mountain people they were known as "granny women." Almost without exception they heralded Mary's news of the proposed midwifery service with interest and even thankfulness. She found in talking with them that most of them had been forced into midwifery in a sincere desire to help neighbors in distress. As one old woman said, somebody had to "cotch" the babies.

Unlike the French midwives whom Mary had known, even the most intelligent of the fifty-three had had no scientific training. They were superstitious and ignorant. To add to the darkness of the picture, there were unfortunately many pseudo-doctors in the mountains. In an extremity the midwives usually appealed to one of them, and many times the situation was worsened, for these so-called doctors were unbelievably ignorant. She even found two such doctors who could neither read nor write.

She was appalled at the tales the midwives told her. Many times healthy young mothers (of fourteen or so) worked at hard physical labor, gave birth to a healthy baby and were back at their work in a matter of hours. But "old" mothers (twenty-two or more) with a history of half a dozen confinements were not always so lucky. If all did not go well, the midwives resorted to spells, herb tea or perhaps an ax—laid edge upward beneath the bed to prevent hemorrhages. They were only too ready to relate to Mary their tales of death, agony and ignorance.

Each day only deepened Mary's desire to make concrete the dream that possessed her, but every nightfall found her stiff and sore from her travels. During the summer she covered 650 miles over primitive mountain trails at an average of three miles per hour.

She went everywhere to find midwives. Most of them lived up the creeks and branches in remote places off the main waterways. Many a night found her at the head of a hollow in surroundings that would have daunted most women, but Mary took it in her stride. In her own words, "I nearly always got a bed to myself."

Plumbing was nonexistent, nor did she expect it. After the inhabitants of the mountain cabin had extended their greetings, she asked for the family washbasin and teakettle. Removing the dirt and grime of the day's journey, she used the remaining hot water to wash out her underwear. Donning the change she carried in her saddlebags, she hung the wet clothing on a bush to dry (rainy nights presented a problem) and was ready for supper with the family. The meal was an occasion for all, for Mary Breckinridge never met a stranger. She was deeply touched by the fact that her host would seldom allow her to pay for her lodging, although the family was living in conditions of dire need.

However, there were brighter spots during the passing of the weeks. Now and then she spent a night at one of the excellent church schools in the hills. Also she met many mountain men and women of means and position who proved to be her lifelong friends and supporters.

By the time Mary met Dr. Woodyard toward the end of the summer, she felt herself to be a seasoned inhabitant of the region. She was ready to introduce her friend to the hills. Dr. Woodyard entered upon her two-week stay with enthusiasm. After she had administered tests to sixty-six children chosen at random from mountain homes, her findings confirmed Mary's opinion that mountain children showed a higher average of intelligence than the national norm.

By the end of the summer Mary Breckinridge knew with certainty that she would return to the Kentucky hills and that Leslie County would be her home. She had even noted a spot of especial beauty on the Middle Fork of the Kentucky River—a high hill whose southern exposure faced towering North Mountain. She intended one day to build her own log house on that hill. With that thought in her mind she bade good-bye to the hill country and set out for the Bluegrass, where she would begin the first lap of the journey that would lead her to the British Isles for her midwifery training.

Now it was autumn of 1923. In the London drawing room of Miss Rosalind Paget, the founder of the Midwives' Institute more than forty years earlier, Mary Breckinridge sat with a cup of tea in her hand and silently blessed the good fortune that had given her an introduction to this pioneer in their common profession of nursing.

The nurse from America reminded herself that at long last she was in England and ready to embark upon the program which she had set for herself in the mountains of Kentucky during the summer just past. She had traveled a long road before she came to that decision. It had begun when she was a child in her father's house in the nation's capital. There she had often heard him and his friends discuss the importance to the country of the men and women who lived close to the soil. Certainly the sturdy, independent Kentucky mountaineers she had encountered on her survey only deepened the conviction she had received so long ago.

Now she watched her silver-haired hostess run a loving hand over the book she herself had just handed her. Mary knew by heart the words on the title page of the small volume with the typically Victorian title. It read:

Introductory Notes
on
Organizing an Institution for Training Midwives
and Midwifery Nurses
by
Florence Nightingale

"It was given to me by Miss Adelaide Nutting, whom I am proud to claim for a friend. Miss Nightingale's cousin gave it to her," Mary explained.

"Miss Nightingale was a very great lady," the older woman said with a little catch in her voice. "I count it a high privilege to have been one of 'Miss Nightingale's Young Ladies', as they called us then. You can hardly imagine the public sentiment fifty years ago against young women of good families going into nursing."

"Some people aren't exactly overjoyed about it now," Mary said dryly. "In my own case, I happen to have had a very understanding father and mother. In addition, I was a bit older than the average probationer, and I made my decision after my husband's death, so I escaped some of the criticism a younger woman might have received. It is a hard life, Miss Paget—but I can't understand why anyone wants to do anything else."

Her hostess smiled. She had recognized at once a

kindred spirit in this clear-eyed, dynamic American woman sitting across from her.

"She has the gift," Rosalind Paget thought. "It is impossible to define, but simple to recognize. Yes, she has the gift."

Aloud she said, "I agree with you, my dear. I have had a great many hardships and stumbling blocks along the road, but if I could choose again, I would not hesitate. I would follow the same road."

Mary's voice held an admiring note. "You have been a nurse for a long time, haven't you, Miss Paget?"

"For many years," the older woman told her. "I received my certificate from the London Hospital in 1879. Some of us soon found out that nurses needed to be midwives as well, so in 1881 we founded the Midwives Institute."

"The year I was born," Mary said.

"The next year I took such training as I could get at the British Lying-In Hospital. I am afraid my co-workers and I shocked the sensibilities of many of our friends and acquaintances. In their minds there were certain menial tasks in nursing which ladies could never do. Even the word 'midwife' was never used in mixed company."

"And because Victorians were like that, thousands of mothers died in childbirth and thousands of children died as infants," Mary said indignantly. "Miss Paget, if you could only know the things I saw in the mountains of Kentucky a few short weeks ago, you wouldn't believe them. It is hard to believe such conditions exist, even in isolated places."

"I know all about them," her hostess assured her. "I began my district work in the poorest part of London, Mary Breckinridge. Ignorance, dirt and superstition are a nurse's foes, no matter where she finds them."

"The people live miles apart in the Kentucky mountains," Mary said. "There are no doctors except for a few in the towns. There are some fine intelligent midwives—although they have no scientific training—but most of them are old and ignorant. There is a great need there. I must do what I can. I have made up my mind to work in the Kentucky mountains the rest of my life if I am needed."

Miss Paget gave her an approving nod. "I knew all about you before you came. That is why I was delighted to see that you be allowed to enroll at the British Hospital for Mothers and Babies in southeast London. We usually call it the Woolwich because it is near the Woolwich Dockyard. You will get the best training in London at the Woolwich, my dear. It made me very happy to recommend you."

Mary was soon hard at work at the British Lying-In Hospital. Since she was already a graduate nurse, her course in midwifery would last for only four months. Untrained women were required to work twelve months in order to obtain certificates.

For Mary time seemed to turn backward; she felt almost like a student nurse again. The matron, Mrs.

Parnell, she regarded with admiration and affection. Mrs. Parnell's father had been a Confederate officer who had come to England after Lee's surrender. Because of his connection with the South, Mary felt a special kinship with his daughter, who as head of the hospital was called Matron according to English custom.

Matron, along with Sister Gregory and Sister Cashmore, ran the hospital. (The nurse from America soon discovered that head nurses and supervisors in England were addressed as Sister.) Mary was to like her three new friends better and better as time went on, but at first she was too occupied fitting into the routine of the hospital to get to know them well.

She found that midwives in training rotated among the mothers' wards, the nurseries, the labor wards, the prenatal clinics and the district. Under a ruling of the Central Midwives Board, each nurse must deliver a minimum of twenty normal cases of childbirth. In addition, the nurses were allowed to watch the abnormal cases as they were delivered by the hospital physician. Also they attended daily medical lectures and classes in midwifery.

Mary soon found her place in the hospital program. The long hours and the hard work mattered little to her. She had crossed the ocean to become a midwife and welcomed each new experience.

But the English climate! A true daughter of the South, she could not accustom herself to the penetrating dampness of the old London hospital. Although her heart went out to the babies when the temperature in the nurseries hovered at a low figure, they did not seem to mind. Dressed in their woolly outfits, they bubbled, gurgled, cooed and wailed like the normal infants they were.

In due time Mary came down with a well-defined case of influenza. Matron, Sister Gregory and Sister Cashmore could not have been more concerned if she had been a member of their own families.

"You must take a week away from the hospital as soon as you are better," Matron told her. "A change of environment will work wonders for you. You can make up the time later."

"I hate to be such a n-n-nuisance," Mary apologized, her teeth rattling like castanets, "b-b-but I think if I could get warm just once, I'd feel b-b-better."

Matron looked tolerantly across the narrow hospital bed at Sister Cashmore and shook her head. "She's having a chill just now, accustomed as she is to central heating. In my opinion, it is a very unhealthful condition, but I find that most Americans insist upon it. Even my own father preferred it."

In a week or so Mary was able to go to Garland's, an old hotel near the Haymarket in downtown London, where she reveled in an open fire replenished at intervals by a little Cockney maid straight out of the pages of Dickens. Mary found herself more exhausted than she had realized. She slept ten or twelve hours every night, but during the day she often visited Miss Paget, whose door was always open to her. Frequently she saw her other English friends. The time passed quickly and soon, restored to health and ready for work again, she was back at the Woolwich.

District duty proved more satisfactory than her period inside the hospital had been. As she walked the narrow courts and winding streets through the rain and fog, she was dressed appropriately in heavy woolens which the dampness did not penetrate. Being warm made the battle with the London fog relatively easy. There were times when she felt almost guilty as she contrasted her adequate clothing with the tattered rags of persons she met in the squalid streets.

She became a familiar figure as she went on her daily rounds. Poverty she found in abundance, but with it a fine British decency. All her life she would remember the dockworkers and their families, especially the babies. If she observed poverty, she learned also the solid dependability of the people themselves. Often she wondered how they developed that quality in the damp rotten houses that sheltered the miserable horde of human beings who spilled over into the streets twice a day on their way to and from work.

Mingling with the East End Cockneys, Mary Breckinridge showed her understanding of human nature. She had a natural instinct that taught her to offer her services without descending to the level of the individuals about her. By simply being among them she seemed to raise their level.

At last the months of training came to an end. Since no nurse was allowed to take her final examinations for a month after her training had ended,

Mary spent some time with a friend at Oxford. After leaving there, she went down to Cornwall, where she reveled for two weeks in the blessings of sun and sea. Again as she had done before, she found her body and mind restored by association with nature. This would occur all her life. To her joy there were great coal fires burning constantly in the country hotel where she stayed in Cornwall. Whenever she came in from a walk along the cliffs that overlooked the sea, the cheer and warmth of the flames on the hearth penetrated to her very bones.

Finally the time came to return to the Woolwich and examinations. These she passed with flying colors, becoming an American certificated English midwife.

But she was not yet ready to begin her work in the mountains of Kentucky. When she had first laid her plans, she had determined to study firsthand the program of the Highlands and Islands Medical and Nursing Service in Scotland and to observe further the midwifery program in England. These goals she intended to realize before she embarked for home to set upon the course she had chosen.

But first she would go back to America for a few months. Her brother Carson and his wife Dorothy, who had married late in 1922, were expecting their first child. They wanted Mary to be there for the great occasion. On April 19, 1924, she sailed for home where she was on hand to greet the newest member of the clan, James Carson Breckinridge, Jr., when he arrived in the world in May.

6 The Outer Hebrides

It was mid-August, 1924. Mary Breckinridge had come to Scotland to study firsthand the famous Highland and Islands Medical Service.

Although she was always eager to see new faces and make new friends, she felt almost a sense of awe as she waited in the Edinburgh office of Sir Leslie MacKenzie, founder and director of the aforementioned organization. She knew that he must be a very important man to be in charge of the government medical and nursing service of all Scotland.

His secretary, a woman with a very businesslike appearance, rose to her feet and opened the door into an inner office.

"Sir Leslie will see you now," she announced.

Mary squared her shoulders and held her head high. It was ridiculous, she told herself, for a forty-three-year-old woman to feel like this. Her father had served his country at the court of the czars. Her grandfather had been Vice-President of the United States and then Secretary of War in the Confederacy. The first John Breckinridge in Kentucky had been the Vice-President of the United States under Jefferson. Certainly her people were not unknown in the nation's annals. She drew herself up to her full height of five feet two inches and advanced with all the dignity she could summon into Sir Leslie Mac-Kenzie's office.

Her fears were groundless. A tall, handsome man in late middle age came to meet her. His rugged features were framed by a magnificent head of graying hair and luxuriant moustaches. Once Mary had seen Samuel Clemens, better known as Mark Twain, and now his image flashed across her mind.

The Scotsman's blue eyes gleamed with amusement. "Why didn't someone tell me you were such a tiny thing?" he exclaimed amusedly. "Why, you are no taller than a girl."

Mary's reserve broke down under his charm. "Back in the South where I come from," she observed tartly, "they don't judge the value of a package by its size."

Her host gave a resounding laugh. "Touché!" he exclaimed. Drawing out a chair, he waved her into it. "Please be seated, Mrs. Breckinridge. You and I have a great deal to talk about. I have been fascinated by your letters in which you tell me that you wish to adapt our services to fit the needs of your Kentucky mountains. Tell me what you plan."

For more than an hour the two sat in his oak-paneled office, while Mary presented her ideas. He listened without saying a word as she spoke, beginning with her Grandmother Lees' interest in needy children of the South, telling about her service in France and finishing with her midwifery training in London. Only once did her voice falter; that was when she spoke of the loss of her own children. Then his eyes shone with sympathy.

"That is all," she finished at last. "Forgive me for taking so much of your time."

"We have only just begun," he assured her.

He walked over to a wall cabinet from which he drew out several maps of varying sizes and shapes. These he spread out before him on a table.

"I suggest you begin your tour of observation in Perthshire," he told her. "The Scottish Board of Health considers their organization a model one. From there—"

He went on speaking, moving his pencil all the while and plotting her route with all the sureness of a commander-in-chief who knows his field of operations perfectly. Mary drank in every word.

Dusk was falling when he gathered up the maps and papers and handed them to her. She smiled up at him. "How can I ever thank you enough, Sir Leslie, for all your help? And now I must be going."

"Not until I deliver a message from my wife," he told her. "She hopes you will dine with us tomorrow night. She will be calling you by telephone at your hotel. You may not be aware that we have a mutual friend in Miss Rosalind Paget. We already know you through her letters, you see."

Mary's eyes shone. "Ah, dear Miss Paget! Due to her kindness and your thoughtfulness, I no longer feel a stranger."

"Nor are you," Sir Leslie assured her. "Friendly people are the same the world over. I think you will find our Highlands and Islands much like your own Kentucky mountains. Our service has proved more than sufficient for us. I trust the one you plan will work for you and yours."

"We will have no Crown grant," she reminded him. "No money from the government to subsidize our work."

"True enough," he nodded. "But you will find a way. People's hearts are big when an appeal is made in the proper way. And you have that way, Mary Breckinridge. Undoubtedly you have that way."

As she rose from her chair, he rose also and shook hands heartily with her. The tall gray-haired Scot and the young-old American nurse had established a friendship that would never be broken.

"I shall be looking forward to tomorrow night," she told him. "My stay thus far in Scotland has proved delightful. I can hardly wait to see the Scottish nursing service in action."

Sir Leslie reached into a desk drawer. "Perhaps this will make your journey easier," he said, handing her a heavy manila-paper portfolio.

Mary took out an official-looking document and stared in disbelief. Stamped in the upper left-hand corner was the royal coat of arms together with the legend, "On His Majesty's Service." She looked at Sir Leslie. He nodded in confirmation.

"We do not issue them indiscriminately," he assured her, "but I think you deserve one. Nurses like you belong not to one country but to that larger fellowship that serves all mankind. Furthermore, although she has not met you yet, my wife and I already regard you as a daughter-in-the-spirit, my dear."

Mary's gray-blue eyes flashed back instant laughter. "You and Lady MacKenzie could not possibly be old enough to be my parents. An older brother and sister, perhaps, but not parents."

Sir Leslie smiled. "Have it your way. At any rate, I am eager for my wife and you to meet."

"It will be my pleasure," she told him. Encouraged by the warmth of his personality, she added, "May I write to you and her from time to time while I am observing the Highlands and Islands Service?"

"Be very sure you do," he told her. With twinkling eyes he reminded her, "You may not always be near a post office. Remember you are going into wild country."

Mary began her investigations to the northwest of Edinburgh in Perthshire, which the Scottish board of health had told her they considered a model county. Some day they hoped to have all shires, or counties, under similar organizations.

She observed with particular interest the fifty-three local committees with their fifty-three midwives functioning under local physicians. Only in the last two years had the magnificently working system with its central director been in operation. Before that time numerous small, frequently overlapping, committees had gone their individual ways with a consequent loss of aim, effort and purpose. Now under the improved conditions each local committee in more or less degree supported itself, the deficit being made up from Crown funds.

Every effort had been made to provide comfortable homelike conditions for the nurse-midwives. In a few instances two nurses occupied a small cottage, with a local girl to prepare their meals. Again a single nurse-midwife would be in lodgings, with her landlady serving her meals in her own cozy quarters.

When there were roads and paths, the nurses rode bicycles. At the edge of the moors they were forced to leave their vehicles and go on foot. As Mary accompanied the superintendent or the assistant superintendent over much of the two thousand miles of Perthshire, she felt more and more at home every day. After all, the name Breckinridge was a Scottish one derived from the wild bracken that stretched for miles on the hills of Scotland. Not too many generations ago her ancestors had lived in this country. As she roamed the wild countryside, she had an intuitive feeling that this, as well as America, was her "ain coun-tree."

From Perthshire she proceeded to Argyll. From there she boarded a small boat bound for the Outer Hebrides, the isolated islands bordering Scotland on the northwest.

Landing finally on the island of Lewis, she traveled twenty-seven miles across the rough countryside in a baker's cart. Here and there as the driver delivered his wares, she found time to visit in one of the "black houses," as the scattered dwellings were called. These primitive places fascinated her. They were built of rough stones gathered from the countryside, with thatched roofs of barley roots and stalks. Many had no windows or chimneys, the smoke from the fire in the center of the room escaping through the roof. It was not difficult to see where the houses derived their names.

For the most part, the men were fishermen. The land yielded poor crops, and most of it was devoted to sheep grazing. Many times Mary saw women carrying heavy loads of peat on their backs. This would be used for fuel in the "black houses."

Although she could not understand the Gaelic spoken by the natives, there was no doubt of the friendliness in their eyes or the welcome in their voices. Often, as she drank strong, scalding tea from an earthen cup while surveying a placid cow in the far end of the building and chickens pecking in the dirt at her feet, she reflected that this mode of living was not too bad. Was it not George Borrow who had said:

There's night and day, brother, both sweet things; sun, moon, and stars, brother, all sweet things; there's likewise a wind on the heath. Life is very sweet, brother; who would wish to die?

Certainly life in this wild, sparsely inhabited land was preferable to existence in the damp, moldy hospital lodgings at the Woolwich, with the slums of

London at one's very doorstep. The people of Lewis knew poverty and deprivation, but they knew also the sweep of sea and sky.

The island houses reminded Mary of the crude log cabins of eastern Kentucky. There, too, the inhabitants were unlettered and ignorant, but they were heirs to the majesty of the mountains. She felt an overpowering eagerness to sail for home and begin her work. But she knew that first she must make a thorough tour of the Hebrides where she could study isolated conditions such as she would meet later in her own country.

Her trip went on by water and by land. Even in the poorest huts she met the hospitality she had experienced in the mountains of Kentucky, and she discovered more than once that an unlettered woman may possess the qualities of a great lady. Before she left Scotland, Mary had acquired fresh ideas and stronger courage to carry out those plans that were becoming more definitive every day.

When her stay in Edinburgh was over, Mary told the MacKenzies and her other Scottish friends good-bye and went on her way to London. Although she was eager to return to America, she knew she had unfinished business to which she must attend.

At an earlier date she had arranged to attend the Post Certificate School, which was affiliated with the York Road Lying-In Hospital. Both were located in the East End of London. Now she was enrolled as a postgraduate student of midwifery. When she began her work in Kentucky with full responsibility as director of a nurse-midwife service, she intended to be as well qualified as it was possible for her to be.

The crowded noisy dirty streets were not new to her, for she had trained at the British Lying-In Hospital, which was also in the East End. Long before that time she had become familiar with the slums of London through the books of Charles Dickens, an author of her childhood whose writing she still loved. And she knew the city from personal experience, for at the age of thirteen she had seen it first with her family. Twice during her years in France she had made short visits to the British metropolis.

Now as she went about the streets on her midwifery cases, she began to feel herself more and more a part of the city, for she served the people both in their suffering and in their joy. Before this time she had been merely a visitor, even in her earlier training days. Now in some undefinable manner she felt that London was *her* city. These people whom she served were *her* people.

In addition to tending her cases on the district, Mary went to lectures at the Royal College of Surgeons and the Midwives Institute. Midwifery and everything relating to it formed the core of her existence.

There were delightful interludes in addition to the work. Sister Turner and Sister Doubleday, her superiors at the Post Certificate School, were deeply dedicated women, but they realized that human beings cannot burn at white heat every moment.

Accordingly they encouraged and even urged Mary to spend her weekends with her friends in London.

Once again the American nurse was a frequent visitor at the old Garland Hotel near the Haymarket. Whenever she made her headquarters there, she often had Sunday night supper with Miss Rosalind Paget, who by now was a fast friend. There were other friendships to renew—Hermione Blackwood, Celia du Sautoy of CARD days, and Miss Peterkin, the Superintendent of the Queen's Institute of District Nursing. The kindness of the last-named permitted Mary to visit the principal center of the institute at Plaistow and watch graduate nurses being taught district nursing, health visiting and midwifery.

Then at Miss Peterkin's suggestion she went on to Hertfordshire to make a study similar to the one she had made earlier in Perthshire. There she made a new friend in Miss Harrington, superintendent of nursing and inspector of midwives in a district numbering more than 300,000 people. All her life, wherever she went, Mary Breckinridge's warm, responsive nature reached out and drew people to her. In Hertfordshire she formed one more tie that would bind her to the British Isles all her life.

The organization in Hertfordshire was an ideal one. The country population numbered more than 300,000 people, with two thirds of them living in small towns and the other third in a rural area. Miss Harrington directed 140 midwives. These women nursed the sick, attended various clinics (school, baby, tuberculosis, etc.), did follow-up work and finally served as midwives to three thousand mothers a year. Qualified physicians held obstetrical and pediatric clinics to supplement the work of the nurse-midwives. From time to time the physicians held medical examinations in the schools. The system was about as perfect as a system could be.

Mary sighed as she wondered if the day would ever come when a similar organization would serve the Kentucky mountains. She knew that insuperable obstacles lay between the present time and the day she would realize her goal. For that very reason she was intensely interested in the Hertfordshire project, especially the financial side. The people in the organization at Hertfordshire seemed to have overcome their stumbling blocks.

There was a voluntary county committee which employed Miss Harrington as superintendent of nurses. The county itself made a grant for her work as inspector of midwives. The educational system paid for nurse service with schoolchildren. Various local organizations did their best to help financially. Patients able to pay anything did so, with fees being scaled to their incomes. There was even an insurance of sorts. Mary's observing eyes saw that although the organization received public aid, its administration was left in the hands of private voluntary groups. "Surely the plan can be adapted to the Kentucky mountains," she told herself.

At the insistence of her old friend, Mrs. Dike, under whose leadership she had instituted the Child

Hygiene and Visiting Nurse Service in the Aisne valley in France, Mary crossed the English Channel to pay a short visit to that country. She traveled in Mrs. Dike's chauffeured car. Although she found that several of her old friends had died, those remaining gave her an overwhelming welcome. In spite of the fact that there had been changes, the roots of the old CARD were still there, and the nurse from America went back to England, secure in the knowledge that the work of her war years had not been wasted.

She had booked passage on the *Rotterdam* for January 14, 1925, but she had the Christmas season to pass in a strange land before that date. Her work in England was virtually finished, and with no duties to fill her time, she felt a restless uneasiness. At seasons such as Christmas when family ties were in the foreground, the children she had lost were never out of her mind. Somehow this year she felt especially lonely.

Then she thought of the sister of her friend, Maud Cashmore, under whom she had trained at the Woolwich. Sister Adeline was an anchoress at the Church of All Saints in York, England. Some years before she had left the world behind and retired to the church in York, where she performed certain menial duties in return for shelter and meager fare. The rest of her time she spent in prayer and devotion.

Mary had met her only once, but at that time she

had been awed by the sister's sense of inner peace. She wished that she, too, possessed it.

Now Christmas, 1924, found the American nurse once more at York. As Sister Adeline gave her a reassuring welcome, Mary's loneliness began to slip away. She spent a memorable twenty-four hours in the shadow of the ancient church where her friend served. Then she told the anchoress good-bye and set out for her hotel where she would spend the night before returning to London in the morning.

But she did not go there at once. Instead she found her way to a street by the river and wandered along the winding Ouse. Wherever she could, she walked along the top of the old wall that had encircled the city since Roman days. Before darkness fell, she visited York Minster and drank in the beauty of its towering heights and fourteenth-century stained glass. She knew she would never forget the spot, but exquisite though it was, she kept a special niche in her heart for the small church where she had attended midnight services the day before.

The hour was growing late as Great Peter, the biggest bell in England, struck solemnly from its position above the west porch between the two bell towers. The six resounding strokes made Mary realize that the day had ended.

Still filled with a serene sense of peace, she turned back toward the hotel. There she found a cheerful fire burning in her room. She pulled the bellrope and an ancient waiter answered the call and set up a little table directly in front of the fire. When he had brought her simple repast, he waited respectfully for a moment.

"Is there anything more, Madam?" he inquired.

She shook her head. "Nothing more, thank you. I think"—she paused and the next words were almost a whisper—"I have everything."

In imagination she could still hear the fresh young voices in the choir at the Church of All Saints singing:

"The King of Love my Shepherd is,
　　Whose goodness faileth never;
I nothing lack if I am His
　　And He is mine forever."

The spirit of that song was the spirit of Sister Adeline—and in some small measure now the spirit of Mary Breckinridge. At last—at long last—she was ready to set in motion the wheels of the nurse-midwifery service that would one day become the Frontier Nursing Service, whose cause she would serve for the rest of her life.

7 The Work Begins

It was May 28, 1925. The lobby of the little Capitol Hotel in Frankfort, Kentucky, was buzzing with activity. Not even during a session of the General Assembly of the commonwealth were there more people coming and going. The hotel was the scene of a meeting called by Mrs. Mary Breckinridge for the purpose of founding the Kentucky Committee for Mothers and Children.

The meeting was under way behind closed doors in the assembly room of the hotel. At Mrs. Breckinridge's request Judge Edward O'Rear, a well-known Kentucky jurist, had opened the meeting, briefly stated its purpose to the audience which included many prominent Kentuckians (and a number of Mary's relatives) and called for an election of officers.

Mary's eyes danced as she looked about her and reflected that more than half the people present were related to her by blood lines or marriage. There was nothing like prolific kin, she thought, to insure the success of an undertaking.

In his opening remarks Judge O'Rear prophesied success for the program because of its "sublime audacity." He said that he knew the mountains because as a young man he had lived in them. His forebears had been a part of them. He liked to think that what the mountain people had to offer was a part of the heritage of America.

"Wherever you find a highland people, they are the seed corn of the world," he said in conclusion.

Mary Breckinridge nodded in confirmation. She felt she had come to know the mountain people, and no one was more aware than she of their solid worth and moral integrity.

The meeting continued. When the election was held, her cousin, Dr. A. J. A. Alexander of Woodford County, was the first chairman, and Mr. C. N. Manning, prominent Lexington banker, the first treasurer. When Dr. Alexander came up on the platform, Mary looked at him proudly. She had a strong feeling for family, and Alex was family. For a few moments she forgot where she was and drifted back in childhood memories. Truly a devious path had led her to this day. Presently her cousin's voice brought her back to her surroundings.

". . . and now I give you Mary Breckinridge, the guiding spirit of the Kentucky Committee," she heard him say.

Slowly she rose to her feet and looked down into the sea of upturned faces before her. They looked so interested, so eager, so loyal—and, bless them, most of them were present because she had asked them to come. She leaned forward a little with her hands resting on the table before her. She talked informally in a conversational tone as though all of them were gathered about her own fireside.

"I can tell you very little you do not already know," she began. "I have been telling the same story over and over ever since I returned from France. I have been telling it with increasing frequency since the summer I spent in the mountains of Kentucky. It was during those months that I made up my mind to spend the rest of my life there in alleviating the unspeakable conditions which have arisen there."

She leaned closer to her audience and waited for a moment. It was an unnecessary gesture, for she already had their full attention.

"Come with me into a region of about a thousand square miles with a population of twenty-nine thousand people," she begged. "It is a wild mountainous land where only three small towns exist. Living is hard. Money is practically nonexistent. The necessities are obtained by sweat and toil or by barter—trading what one has for what one wants. More often one simply does without. There are no telephones, few roads, no electricity, no indoor bathrooms. Since these people know nothing of modern science and sanitation, the death rate is extremely high. There are not more than three or four doctors in the entire region, and they cannot begin to serve the people, who for the most part live in remote cabins and shacks far up the rivers and creeks in the hills. Their enemies are ignorance, dirt, disease, superstition—and death."

A low murmur ran through the crowd, but intent upon her message, Mary went on:

"Friends, you need not imagine such a region. It is there in Leslie County, Knott County and Owsley County where I propose with your help to carry on a nursing-midwife service. It will have a double purpose. It will save lives in the mountains of Kentucky. If it is successful—and I promise you it will be—it will be a beacon to forgotten frontiers not only in our own United States but all over the world. Frankly, I expect nurse volunteers to come to us from the far corners of the earth."

In the audience heads nodded knowingly and confident smiles were exchanged. Here was evidence of the "sublime audacity" to which Judge O'Rear had made reference.

"In America the death rate for women in childbirth," Mary Breckinridge continued, "is the highest in the civilized world. Every year we lose nearly two hundred thousand babies at birth or in the first month of life, as well as nearly twenty thousand mothers. We have lost more mothers in childbirth than men in all the wars we have fought."

A shocked undercurrent went through the assembled people. The speaker before them had aroused their interest and stirred their sympathies.

"In 1923," she informed them, "the mortality rate among fifty-four thousand, five hundred and fifty-four confinements attended by nurses of the Queen's Jubilee Institute was one point four per thousand. In England midwives *know* how to meet emergencies. They *know* what to do until the doctor comes. In most cases, they never have to call the doctor, for prenatal care has insured safe deliveries. If England and Scotland can have such a service, why can't we? I am here to tell you that we can. The presence of so many friends and relatives here today heartens me more than I can ever tell you. Let us waste no more time, but take the first steps to launch our program."

Before the meeting had ended, the members had provided for an annual audit, accurate records, transportation of patients to the nearest city for hospital care, with E. B. Jouett, a member of the committee and an officer of the Louisville and Nashville Railroad, promising to supply free passes, the status of midwives, an honorary membership for the state health officer, and full powers for the executive group of the Kentucky Committee for Mothers and Babies. (The name was not changed to the Frontier Nursing Service until 1928.)

Long before the meeting at the Capitol Hotel had taken place, Dr. Arthur McCormick, the state health officer, had impressed upon Mary Breckinridge the necessity for obtaining and keeping accurate records so that the nursing-midwives service would have a valid basis of comparison. During the course of the meeting it was decided to have a regularly printed report on the work of the committee. This was the nucleus of the Frontier Nursing Service *Quarterly Bulletin.* Mrs. Breckinridge was editor as long as she lived.

The committee decided to employ Miss Bertram Ireland of Scotland, who was at the present time in the United States, to conduct in the area chosen by the committee a survey of births and deaths which had occurred since 1911, the time at which registration of those vital statistics had become legal in Kentucky. Miss Ireland had been recommended to Mrs. Breckinridge by no other than Sir Leslie MacKenzie himself.

The final act of the Frankfort meeting was to approve unanimously Miss Linda Neville's motion to employ Miss Freda Caffin and Miss Edna Rockstroh as nurse-midwives. Both were experienced public-health nurses completing midwifery training in England at the time of the Kentucky meeting.

The members of the committee left the Assembly Room with the satisfied feeling of a job well begun. As the crowd filed out through the double doors, Mrs. Breckinridge sank down into the nearest chair in the almost vacant room. Only Dr. Alexander and Dr. McCormick remained with her.

"I can't believe it has really happened," she sighed. "At last we are on our way. With what those dear people who pay into the treasury and with what others have already given, there are sufficient funds to pay for the summer's work. I feel there is something almost symbolic about the thousand dollars of Grandmother Lees's money which I gave in memory of my mother, the hundred dollars from Aunt Jane and the fifty dollars from Mrs. Dike. Hazelwood, Kentucky and France are launching my dream."

"Your dream will cost a pretty penny before it is fulfilled," Dr. McCormick warned her.

Alex Alexander laid a hand affectionately on his cousin's shoulder. "Mary will raise the money somehow," he told Dr. McCormick. He smiled down at her. "After all, she has underwritten the work for the next three years."

"I told you not to tell that," Mrs. Breckinridge scolded. "To be sure, I hope the money will come in from gifts and donations, but meanwhile the work must go on. You two men must promise to keep my part a secret, or I shall be very angry with you both."

Mary Breckinridge gave "Ireland of Scotland" her unqualified approval from the first. The young woman proved to be all that Sir Leslie had claimed. She set to work with a will to survey the 376 square miles of Leslie County, where the Frontier Nursing Service planned to make its start. There were creeks to cross, rivers to ford, trails to follow. Armed with a map printed by the geological survey department of the state, she set out alone on horseback.

Mrs. Breckinridge soon realized that the nurse must have help if the job was to be finished by the end of the summer. Miss Zilpha Roberts, a schoolteacher and also a native of Leslie County, offered to accompany her. When the two nurse-midwives, Freda Caffin and Edna Rockstroh, arrived, they also were assigned to Miss Ireland. Two more helpers were added by Miss McCord at the Wooten Community Center.

If there was a family Bible in a cabin, the work

was simple. But too many times the persons interviewed looked in vain for a lost scrap of paper or a tattered composition book in some old box or trunk. Sometimes the questioners had to seek out some other member of the family. In a section of the country where clocks and calendars were rare, the records, if kept at all, were not too reliable.

Bertram Ireland and her co-workers were in a wild land. They listened to old-timers' tales of wildcats springing from overhanging limbs at night on luckless travelers. They met snakes as they rode along lonely paths. One day when she was on foot, Miss Ireland stepped on a long snake, which wriggled away. The snake moved fast, and she moved faster. To her horror she stepped on it again. As she wrote later, she "danced a jubilee on that old snake all the way down the mountain."

But there were also compensations. When the mountain people understood what the nurses were trying to do, they almost overwhelmed them with appreciative attention.

An unkempt-looking man at the head of a hollow said to Miss Ireland, "It's a rough country, ma'am, and we're a poor people, but there aren't a cleverer on the face of the earth."

As they rode down the trail from the mountain cabin, Bertram Ireland turned a puzzled face to Zilpha Roberts. "Cleverer? Now what did he mean by that?"

The mountain teacher laughed. "He was using the

word in its old sense—generous—hospitable—ready to help."

"I'll accept that," her companion agreed. "They are the kindest people in the world *after* they decide to trust you, but you must prove yourself trustworthy first."

While the six workers were collecting data concerning births and deaths, Mary Breckinridge was hard at work, riding the length and breadth of Leslie County. Everywhere she went she was careful to select the leading citizens for the branch committee. She copied what she had seen in the British Isles, where the nursing service always included local personnel.

She found the days pleasant in spite of hardships in travel and crude accommodations at night. The summer she had spent in the saddle two years ago made her feel at home in the mountains now. One old grizzled mountaineer passed judgment on her as she rode away from his family's cabin where she had stayed the night.

He spoke gruffly, but his voice was warm: "Why, she's jest folks same as us."

Spurred on by her purpose and pleased by the welcome from friends she had made two years ago, she used to good advantage her gift of organization. Being Mary Breckinridge, she managed at the same time to give nursing care to sick babies and suggestions on child rearing to eager mothers as she rode from spot to spot.

A heart-warming interlude occurred during mid-summer. A letter from her brother Clif, now Captain Breckinridge, set his sister to preparing for his home-coming. For a few weeks she thrust all thought of work from her and visited with her younger brother at the home of cousins in Woodford County. In order to reunite the young soldier with his kin, she rented a country club near Lexington for a family party to which she invited nearly a hundred guests. There Clif met Martha Prewitt, a distant cousin who was one day to become his wife.

On August 22, 1925, the Leslie County Committee held its initial meeting in the courthouse at Hyden. Thirty-five members were present, among them the outstanding members of the community. Several state officers arrived for the purpose of taking the local committee into the group.

An air of excitement pervaded the little mountain town. Outside visitors did not come every day. Evidently the summer work was bearing fruit. The collectors of statistics had made many friends for the nursing-midwives service, and the mountain people who knew Mary Breckinridge had already given her their hearts and trust.

The day proved a gala one. All the outstanding people of Leslie County were present. The county superintendent of schools made a speech. The editor of the weekly newspaper made another. As for Judge L. D. Lewis, who was to prove a lifelong friend of the nursing service and its director, he buzzed about as though the whole idea were his own and beamed warmly on Mrs. Breckinridge and everyone connected with her.

Meanwhile the Leslie County committee set in motion the wheels of the organization that would in a few years set the little town on the map and gain it world renown. From their own number the committee elected officers to direct their future plans.

Every citizen of Hyden was well aware that big things were under way. They were proud of their town, proud of the new organization and proud of Mary Breckinridge. Once again she had received a vote of confidence from the mountain people.

8 The First Christmas

The Frontier Nursing Service established temporary headquarters in an old ramshackle two-story building, the only vacant one in Hyden. It provided living space for the director and the two nurses in addition to a one-room dispensary and a nearby barn for the horses.

"At least it's decent," Mary pronounced. "The conveniences can come later."

When the first clinic was opened in September, 1925, the little dispensary was well stocked with typhoid serum, smallpox vaccine, croup kettles, hypodermic needles, baby scales and other necessities. While the care of mothers and babies was Mary's chief concern, it went hand in hand with public-health nursing, which she knew must be carried on. Already she had made several trips down from the mountains to the Bluegrass country in order to secure supplies and attend to the thousand and one details which demanded her attention.

While the day-to-day work of the Frontier Nursing Service went on, Mary Breckinridge turned her efforts in yet another direction. Earlier in 1925 she had bought the land up Middle Fork which on her first trip to Kentucky she had determined to make her own. Soon Big House and its surrounding buildings began to take shape.

A contractor in Hazard, twenty-five miles away, agreed to ride over from time to time and oversee the work. Mary watched the construction of Big House with poignant eagerness whenever she could escape from her rapidly expanding duties. From the very first she could envision the large two-story log house with great stone fireplaces and chimneys built by men who had learned the craft from their fathers and they in turn from their fathers as far back as the days when Kentucky was a wilderness. Except for briefings from the contractor, no outside help was needed until the time came to install the plumbing and finish the exterior.

Meanwhile the headquarters at Hyden had taken on an air of semi-permanency. The work of the nursing-midwife service progressed steadily. Miss Caffin and Miss Rockstroh made their daily rounds on horseback with Mrs. Breckinridge accompanying them in case of an emergency. Inoculations were given against the ever-present typhoid, gunshot wounds were treated and minor illnesses were cared for.

Mrs. Caffin, the mother of one of the nurses, joined the group at Hyden and became a volunteer housekeeper. The next person to arrive was Mary's seventy-nine-year-old father, Clifton Breckinridge. He brought with him his fox terrier Patch, a gift to Breckie years ago. In spite of his age Mr. Breckinridge was in excellent health. He filled his days by finding things to do that contributed to the nursing project. Not only did he make small repairs wherever he found they were needed, but he groomed and cared for the nurses' horses as well.

However, his greatest contribution lay in becoming a member of the Hyden Committee, where he soon became almost as well loved as his daughter. There was no doubt that the hardy men and women of the mountains took particular pride in the fact that one of their number had rubbed shoulders with crowned heads of Europe and taken part in a storied pomp that seemed to them almost like a fairy tale. In addition, Clifton Breckinridge was a valued member in his own right, for he was a natural leader in any group.

The organization family was enlarged when Juliette Carni, with her husband Henri and Liliane, a daughter by a former marriage, came to join Mary once more. Juliette had been Breckie's nurse, and Mary had always loved her dearly for that reason. The two women decided that they would work together from now on. Juliette became cook-housekeeper, with Liliane as her first assistant. Henri was the barn man. They moved into a new cabin on the Middle Fork as soon as it was ready and invited the contractor to stay with them so that he could spend more time on the building site.

The days passed in a busy confusion of conferences with workmen, routine visits on horseback and attention to any and everything that arose. Mary Breckinridge thanked God for a strong, sturdy body, for after a day on horseback she frequently found herself spending half the night at her ancient type-writer. There were orders to make out, bills to pay, and letters to write to a widening circle of friends of the nursing-midwives service, acquainting them with the problems of today and the needs of tomorrow.

After she and Teddy Bear, a horse which she had purchased in the Bluegrass country, became lost for a short time one winter's afternoon on a snow-topped mountain, Mary realized that time was passing and Christmas was drawing near. In a few months she would move into Big House, as she had decided to call the log building under construction up the river from Hyden, and at last have a home all her own. For a fleeting moment she remembered last year, Sister Adeline and the peace and serenity that had been hers since those Christmas hours with her friend in York.

"I wish the upstairs at Big House were finished," she said aloud to her father. "I would love to invite everybody in Leslie County to a Christmas dedication."

"That would be a right sizable party," Mr. Breckinridge told her. "The population is about ten thousand."

Mary nodded. "I know, Father. Well, after all, who needs an upstairs for a party? I am going to invite all ten thousand and give our mountain children a day they will never forget. I am sure the friends of the nursing service will supply the gifts."

Clifton Breckinridge's eyes twinkled. "I daresay

they won't all come. Nevertheless, you can't ask people to a party without making plans for feeding them. Now how in the world do you expect to feed ten thousand cold and hungry people? The weather is bound to be cold, and of course they will be hungry."

Mary's eyes twinkled in return. "I'll make a deal with you, Father. I will see to getting the toys and candy for the children if you and Juliette will take care of the food. Agreed?"

Mr. Breckinridge nodded with enthusiasm. "Agreed. Now Juliette and I will get on with the planning."

He drew an old envelope from his coat pocket and began to make notes on matters he wished to talk over with the Swiss woman. He had already decided to purchase enough smoked hams to feed their guests. Meanwhile Mary made lists of friends and relatives who would help her get the necessary toys and candy. Soon she had a circular in the mail, telling of her plans and appealing for money and supplies. As she anticipated, the response to her request was heart-warming.

The women on the Hyden Committee together with Juliette baked ham and homemade bread until the wonderful smells that emanated from their kitchens seemed to hover over the little town. Puddings and cakes were included on the bill of fare, and a new wash boiler was ordered in which to make the cocoa.

The men of the local committee used their mule teams to haul the toys, candy and other supplies from the post office at Hyden to Big House. The women in the community freshened up doll clothes and made new wardrobes for the dolls that needed them. These same women joined in sacking the candy.

A few days before Christmas the carpenters stopped their labor so that preparations for the party could get full speed ahead. The new floor at Big House was swept until it was spotless. Festoons of greenery and holly decorated the walls. The huge logs in the stone fireplace awaited only the touch of a match.

But the crowning glory of it all was the great fir tree towering up to the ceiling in the center of the spacious living room. It was decorated with ornaments and tinsel sent from the Bluegrass. There were no lights, for there was no electricity, and Mary refused to have candles because of the ever-present danger of fire.

Since the party would be a daytime affair, the lights would not be missed. Mary knew that the shining tree with its many colored ornaments would seem like a miracle anyway to the wide-eyed children who would cluster around it. Her own eyes lighted with anticipation as she imagined them stretching out their hands for the gifts already piled high about the tree. Only yesterday at Hyden she had seen a child with a make-believe doll fashioned from a bit of blanket with a stone for its head. That little girl would have a real doll. Mary intended that this party should stand out in her young guests' minds for years to come.

But Christmas Day dawned cold and bleak. The

river was running high. Not all the ten thousand invited guests came; she had not expected them. However, about five hundred brave hearty souls put in their appearance. They came on foot, on mule-back, on horseback and in wagons, buggies and surreys.

At first young and old trooped shyly into Big House, where logs blazed in the great fireplace and the silver tinsel on the tree reflected the dancing sparkling flames on the hearth. The Christmas tree ornaments could not outshine the bright eyes of the children who looked for the first time at a sight they could not possibly have imagined.

From the candy and toys stacked high at the base of the tree, each child chose something that caught his fancy. Every little girl wanted a doll of her own to cuddle, but the supply was exhausted all too soon. The candy and toys lasted longer.

At last the giving of gifts was over. Now began the part of the day which Mary had planned from the beginning. At a given signal a choir of boys and girls from Hyden sang "Come All Ye Faithful," followed by "O Little Town of Bethlehem" and "Silent Night." A curious quiet fell upon the assembled guests as the fresh young voices rang out.

When the Hyden minister finished his prayer, her good friend Judge Lewis spoke, and after him Clifton Breckinridge. Then Mary rose and looked into the faces of the people gathered there.

She reminded them that she had regarded them as friends ever since she first came among them to do work for them and their children in memory of her own little son and daughter. She knew that she belonged in the mountains, and she was grateful to them for accepting her as one of their own. With the conclusion of her words, the day came to an end.

Long before dark the guests started homeward, for travel in the mountains was not safe after nightfall. Finally the last child had departed, a toy or a doll clutched tightly, the last guest had said goodbye, the last echoing footstep had died away in Big House. The log house was very still, for even Mary Breckinridge was on her way back to her lodgings at Hyden.

But the flickering flames upon the hearth in the long living room cast lights and shadows upon the bronze plaque built into a corner of the great stone chimney:

> TO THE GLORY OF GOD
> AND IN MEMORY OF
> BRECKIE AND POLLY
> DEDICATED CHRISTMAS 1925

After the dedication of Big House Mary immediately began to make plans to go to New York. She had been invited to hold meetings in the homes of Anne Morgan and Elizabeth Perkins in the East, where she could meet their friends and tell them about the progress of their work.

The time had come when it was necessary to consider hiring a secretary. Just before leaving for the East, Mary attended the executive meeting in Lexington on December 30, 1925. At this meeting she

was "empowered to employ a secretary, in the event
that funds are secured to justify the expense." She
never doubted that the funds would be forthcoming,
for they were already pouring in, not only from Kentucky but also from the large eastern cities where she
had previously spoken. Her invitations were increasing so rapidly that the services of a secretary to keep
track of her engagements alone had become a necessity.

Her visit to New York in January, 1926, was the
first of the six- to twelve-week trips that Mary made
from that time on each year. The subscriptions that
came in as a result of her meetings in the homes of
friends, in churches and in clubs came from people
who gave willingly and generously—people who
wished to share with Mary some of the exultation
she was experiencing as she worked with mothers,
babies and older children in an isolated and remote
area.

In these early meetings she did not ask for money.
In the first place she disliked appealing to a captive
audience. It was her belief that donations came in as
freely and perhaps even more generously when the
donors caught some of the sparkling enthusiasm
with which she recounted her experiences and told
her plans.

By spring Mary had begun to furnish Big House.
She culled what she thought most practical from the
family possessions in a fireproof storage house in
Louisville. These things included some furniture,
one oriental rug for the living room, some of her

mother's bed linens and of course many of the books
with which she had grown up. For Mary Breckinridge a house was not a home until there were books
in it. She purchased draperies and china which were
in keeping with the rustic surroundings.

Although Big House was well named, it soon became a crowded one. Until Hyden Hospital was built
three years later, it served also as a hospital. A sick
child brought to Mary's home for treatment might
stay on for weeks if his home conditions were not
good. Confinement cases were often cared for there
for the same reason. From time to time, additional
beds were set up in every available nook and cranny.

People who came and went up and down the river
often stopped off to enjoy a meal or take a bath.
Mary said once, with her eyes twinkling in their
usual manner, that it might be well to keep a guest
book in the downstairs bathroom because so many
people availed themselves of the use of the bathtub.
At that time there were only five bathtubs in all Leslie County; two of them were in Big House.

During these years all who were entertained or
cared for at Big House were Mary's guests. All their
names were in the handsome guest book which Ireland of Scotland had presented to her hostess.

Not every nurse who arrived to work in the nursing service during its first year had received training
as a midwife. There was a need for general nursing,
especially to take care of diphtheria and typhoid
inoculations and treatment for those diseases. Dr.
McCormick, state health director, issued licenses to

practice midwifery to those nurses who had received this postgraduate training. But not enough of them were available to take care of their work and also of the diseases which were endemic to the region. Mary had plans for the future when general nurses who liked midwifery would be sent to England for further training. She was making plans also in another area of the nurses' training.

Learning to ride a horse was not included in the regular training course for nurses. Nor was it included in the postgraduate course of midwifery which many of the early nurses who came to the Kentucky mountains had completed. Mary soon realized when her new aides began arriving that a nurse's bravery and ingenuity, even in dealing with death, did not carry over into her riding.

This fact was forcibly brought home to Mary on the day when she met Ellen Halsall, the first nurse-midwife to come to Big House, at the railroad station in Hazard.

After getting the new arrival on the horse's back and placing the reins in her cold hands, Mary instructed the nurse to follow her down the creek bed. She failed to note the startled look, as well as the increasing pallor, on the girl's face.

Before they had proceeded far, Mary heard a strangled call for help. She turned and saw that her new nurse had slipped in her saddle to a somewhat horizontal position on the horse's side. She was holding onto the saddle with one hand and with the other she was clutching the reins so violently that her mount was turning round and round in circles.

Mary hurried to her rescue before Ellen hit the ground. Then she took the reins and straightened the poor girl to an upright position.

"Everything will be fine if only you will just sit quietly in the saddle and hold the reins loosely," she assured the newcomer.

The girl looked unconvinced, but made an effort to do as her mentor said.

Mary again rode ahead. "Follow me," she called back over her shoulder. "Try to do as I do."

For a few minutes all seemed well, and they rode along in silence. Then there was another choked call for help. Turning quickly, Mary saw the neophyte equestrian, her eyes bulging, with a death grip on the reins. The patient animal she was riding had about reached his limit. He was waltzing about on his hind legs, and Mary fancied his eyes were bulging, too. The tightly drawn reins threatened to turn him over backward.

Again Mary rushed to the nurse's aid. She reached for the reins—and the horse quickly lowered his forelegs to the ground.

Mary stifled a smile. "Just hold onto the saddle, my dear," she told Ellen. "I'll lead your horse the rest of the way."

Over the mountains and across the valleys the travelers continued the rest of their twenty-five-mile journey. Mary spent most of the time considering what all nurses new to the mountains must learn. She determined that from this day forward all arrivals would take at least five riding lessons before they started their work.

As for Ellen Halsall, her thoughts ran along different lines. She was trying hard to remember why Richard III had ever shouted: "A horse! A horse! My kingdom for a horse!" As far as the young nurse was concerned, she felt the quadruped was greatly overrated.

9 Out by Boat

During the first year the nurse-midwives services grew by leaps and bounds. Immediately after the Christmas party and dedication of Big House in December, 1925, Mary Breckinridge traveled out of the mountains to meet with committees in the East.

The movement was spreading and her work was increasing. While the executive committee in Lexington, in December, 1925, had voted that she be empowered to employ a secretary, it remained for the right person to appear. On her way back from the East to the mountains a few months later, she asked her young kinswoman, Martha Prewitt, if she would accept the job. When the latter accepted with enthusiasm, Mrs. Breckinridge felt a load had dropped from her shoulders.

With her new secretary she moved into Big House before it was completed. Surrounded by the family furniture and books, she felt at once a peculiar sense of permanency and belonging. No matter how many times she might travel out of the mountains on business for the nursing service, Big House would be waiting for her when she returned.

To Mrs. Dike in England she wrote: "I am beginning to commute between Lexington, Louisville and the mountains. During the last two months I have gone in and out on an average of every ten days and as that means nearly a day in the saddle and a night on the sleeper each time, you can see that it is tall commuting."

The summer of 1926 proved a busy one for Mary, who continued to ride in and out of the centuries. Although the trips outside were necessary, she always looked forward to the peace of the hills, the long ride on horseback to Big House and its welcoming shelter at the end of the journey.

This year brought Gladys Peacock whom Mrs. Breckinridge had known in France. With her was a Texas nurse, Mary B. Willeford, better known as Tex, who had trained in London at the York Road Lying-In Hospital. As their director, Mrs. Breckinridge lost no time in giving them a special assignment.

Mrs. Draper Ayer of Boston had given funds for building an outpost nursing center (to be known as the Jessie Draper Preston Memorial Nursing Center) at Beech Fork. Tex and Peacock had been in Kentucky only two months when Mrs. Breckinridge sent for them one morning.

"I want you to go to Beech Fork, build the nursing center and open up the district," she told them.

"Build a house!" they chorused.

"Mrs. Breckinridge, do you know what you just said?" Tex inquired.

"We don't know anything about building," Peacock protested.

"Neither did I when I began Big House," Mary Breckinridge told them crisply. "Your job shouldn't be too bad. I have ordered a ready-built house to be delivered at Pineville. From there it will be hauled to Beech Fork."

"We—" began Tex.

"Yes?" With slightly uplifted eyebrows the director looked at her coolly.

Tex left her sentence unfinished. "Come on, Peacock," she said grimly to the other girl. "We are about to make history."

Mrs. Breckinridge's eyes twinkled with amusement as she looked at the straight backs of the departing nurses. She had learned early that one must be very firm with these wonderful young people.

Half an hour later the two nurses were on their way to Beech Fork. In spite of their overwhelming assignment, they were gay and lighthearted.

"Do you know I believe that Kermit Morgan is right," Tex told her companion, as she gave her horse a loose rein.

"How is that?" the English girl asked.

"He says that if Mrs. Breckinridge tells you to do something, you do it whether you can or not."

Peacock and Tex took up their labors in a state of blissful ignorance. They went about their professional work on the district with the confidence and assurance of accomplished midwives. However, when they returned for the day from their rounds, they had other roles to play. There was the building to be supervised and a local committee to set up. At night they stayed with a friendly family nearly three miles away from the building site.

Every few weeks Mrs. Breckinridge rode up river on Teddy Bear. It always gave the resident nurses a lift to see the familiar figure in the gray-blue uniform (adapted from that of CARD days) on the big Bluegrass horse.

She approved the block foundation on which the house would rest, commended the nurses for the friendly rapport they had established with the building foreman and sympathized with them over the problems they had in getting the prefabricated house hauled from the railroad at Hazard.

"Twenty-four-mule-team wagons!" Gladys Peacock groaned. "Who would have thought a small house could possibly have that much material in it?"

"Twenty-two miles!" Tex chimed in.

Mrs. Breckinridge looked thoughtfully at the piles of lumber stacked beside the half-raised walls. Having been through the ordeal of seeing Big House rise foot by foot, she knew that the new nursing center was far from finished.

"Perhaps in the future it will be better to forget the prefab idea," she acknowledged.

"Oh, yes!" Tex clasped her hands in a mockingly suppliant attitude. "Every board has to be mitred to fit the one next to it. The men are really good sports, but I think they are getting frustrated. I know I am. Don't ever trust directions that sound so simple. You can't believe them."

Before the house was completed, rock for the

chimney had to be hauled several times. After the solid oak barn was built, it was roofed with hand-hewn shingles. Further headaches were caused by the installation of a septic tank and a drainage field, but at last with the help of a man from Hyden the plumbing was put in. Finally the nursing center was ready for occupancy.

Then Peacock and Tex set the date for a house-warming. People came from miles around. Of course Mrs. Breckinridge was there and looked on approvingly as various workmen pointed out their respective parts in the construction of the center.

"It will be much easier for you to build the next one," she told the two nurses.

"Wh-hat do you mean?" Peacock asked weakly.

"She means it will be much easier for us to build the next one," Tex echoed.

The corners of Mrs. Breckinridge's mouth twitched uncontrollably. "Surely you don't think I intend to allow all this valuable experience to go down the drain, do you?"

Perhaps it was as well for the nurses' peace of mind at that moment that they did not know they would superintend the building of four more centers. But all that lay in the future.

The task of seeing the next nursing center started and finished fell to Ellen Halsall, who by this time had become a satisfactory rider. Many times in the early days as Mary Breckinridge rode horseback from Krypton, where she left the train from the Bluegrass and proceeded on her way to Hyden, she

looked at the steep mountains and thought that few
people could live on the slopes. But she was wrong.
From the days of the opening of the Frances Bolton
Center at Possum Bend, the nursing midwifery service there included more than a thousand people.

But the nursing center did not materialize over
night, although the eager citizens raised pledges to
the amount of five hundred dollars, a large sum of
money in a country where the main medium of ex-
change was still barter. The chairman of the local
committee gave three acres of good land on which to
locate the center. The Frontier Nursing Service was
fortunate enough to secure the services of an experienced builder who was spending his vacation in his
home town.

When Ellen Halsall opened up the new district,
she took up residence, along with a young mountain
girl as housekeeper and a hefty bull terrier for pro-
tection, in a small one-room cabin on the banks of
the river.

Mary Breckinridge set her seal of approval on
their arrangements the first time she occupied the cot
they had set aside for her visits. Even these temporary quarters, which served while the real center was
under construction, had the air of simple cheerful-
ness characteristic of all the outposts as they grew.

"It's not every nurse who can have decorations
used for a queen's visit," Mrs. Breckinridge said,
with a wave of her hand at the full yellow curtains
separating the living quarters from the dispensary.

A friend of the nursing service had obtained yards

and yards of yellow cotton used for decorative pur-
poses during the recent visit of Queen Marie of
Romania to Louisville. Some of it had found its way
to Possum Bend, and even the cots had spreads of
the gay fabric.

"I wouldn't change places even with a queen,"
Ellen said loyally. "However, I'm glad to share her
yellow cotton."

In mid-November the rain began to fall in tor-
rents. Within an unbelievably short time the river
began to leave its banks.

"We'd better get out of here while we can, Miss
Halsall," the young housekeeper warned. "That ol'
river is gettin' powerful wild."

Ellen looked out the window at the rushing water
bearing logs and other debris swiftly past. One winter at Wendover had been enough to warn her that
the Middle Fork, mild as a lamb in summer days,
could become as fierce as a tiger. She turned away
and nodded to Dolly.

"Let's pack," she agreed. "The dispensary supplies must be packed first. We can carry big loads on
the horses if we are careful."

The young women made three trips up to the new
center before they moved the barest personal necessities. They looked back as they made the last trip up
the steep hill where the comfortable white house
stood on a bluff high above the rushing muddy
water.

"Well, there's one thing sure," Dolly announced
as she held the door of their new house open for

Ellen, who staggered in with an armload of bed-clothes, pillows, sweaters, and miscellaneous articles.

"What's that?" the nurse inquired, wiping off her damp forehead.

The other girl looked at the river rushing far below the point where their new outpost was built and laughed. "That ol' devil water'll never get up here."

The third outpost, the Clara Ford Nursing Center, was built on Red Bird River in Clay County in 1928. Again Peacock and Tex were in charge. They moved over from Beech Fork in July to occupy a two-room cabin while the log house given by Mrs. Henry Ford was being built. As an extra generous touch, she added an electric-light plant.

The nurses were almost swamped with their district work from the beginning. During the first nine weeks they delivered two babies and registered nine more expectant mothers. They gave almost fourteen hundred shots for typhoid and diphtheria. They held clinics for babies and toddlers. Several times they were forced to send to Manchester, the county seat, for physicians. In addition, they found time to organize the local committee.

"Thank heaven, the Ford Motor Company is interested in the center," Tex moaned one night as she dropped wearily into bed. "It would be just too much to watch everything put together piece by piece as we did with that awful prefabricated job."

Peacock laughed. "You'll have to admit it turned out all right. But never again—I hope."

But the day-to-day program of the nurses of the Frontier Nursing Service was not so dramatic as the building of the centers. More would follow in due time, but the work of Mary Breckinridge's nurses never stopped.

While Peacock and Tex superintended the building of the first one in the summer of 1926, the other district nurses had gone on about their neighborhood duties, giving prenatal care, delivering babies and checking later to see that all had gone well. But they did far more than that. Typhoid and dysentery were rampant. Smallpox and diphtheria were also present. Later in the year these plagues would be followed by pneumonia and influenza.

The nurses rode up and down the dry creek beds, inoculating well people with typhoid serum and caring for those who already had the disease. Since these inoculations were necessary to guard against typhoid, the nurses were forced to go back and forth to many points four and five times, for on each trip individuals appeared who had not been there before. To the nurses, as to their director, Big House with its lights at all the windows shone out like a beacon in the night when they returned home at the end of a difficult, dangerous journey.

A special visitor came that summer of 1926. Aunt Jane, Mary's paternal aunt, accompanied by her grandson Brooke Alexander, came in a mule-drawn wagon from Krypton with Mary riding along on Teddy Bear like a guard of honor. The old lady endured the jolting and tipping of the wagon with true

Breckinridge aplomb until they finally came in sight of Big House. Then she gave a deep sigh of relief.

Mary laughed. "Poor Aunt Jane!"

The wagon had reached the foot of the hill. Mary's relative forgot her discomfort as she looked up at the big log house above. The usual country sounds drifted down to her. A horse whinnied in the barn. Juliette's great watch dog gave a deep bark from the kitchen regions as the front door of Big House opened. Clifton Breckinridge with the fox terrier Patch dancing on ahead started down the long steps to greet his sister. Smoke curled up from the kitchen chimney.

"Why, it's home!" Aunt Jane exclaimed delightedly.

Mary threw her an affectionate glance. "I'm glad you feel that way. I've been hoping you'd find a name for the place—a good old British name to match the mountain people with their British heritage. After some travelers have made the trip across the mountains, they insist it should be called Scramble-Over."

"Scramble-Over—Scramble-Over." Suddenly Aunt Jane's eyes lighted up. "I have it. Wend-over— Wendover—Wendover, Mary. There's a name for you."

Fourteen-year-old Brooke, who had been Breckie's playmate in the long-ago days, soon proved himself invaluable in helping to care for the horses and taking them to the railroad to meet incoming nurses and visitors. Mary and he occupied two tents on the slope below Big House because the place was running over with guests, resident nurses and patients. At first Mary's heart was heavy with the thought that another fair-haired boy might have been there with him if a cruel fate had not intervened. Then she resolutely put the thought from her and enjoyed her young kinsman's companionship as she enjoyed that of all adolescents.

She was happy to have her Aunt Jane at Wendover for the summer. Because she had a strong feeling for family, she always felt a distinct lift when she returned from a hard day on the district or a long tiresome ride from the railroad to find her aunt and her father walking placidly together with Patch trotting on ahead.

The two loved the property as though it were their own. Aunt Jane paid for an addition to the sturdy barn, and Clifton Breckinridge occupied himself with directing the terracing of the steep slopes and holding them with stone walls to prevent their washing down into the valley when hard rains came.

The month of December, 1926, brought torrential rains. Roads that had been none too good were now washed out. The U. S. mail was held up, and Christmas supplies were stranded at the railroad. There would be no Christmas celebration at Wendover this year, for travel was impossible. The nurses at Hyden, Wendover and the Jessie Draper Preston outpost were completely isolated by the flood waters that thundered down the valleys carrying logs, trees and even tons of earth which had been torn away in landslides.

The nurses planned to celebrate Old Christmas on January 6, if they could manage to travel and get together. Meanwhile they fought their way along slippery trails and across hazardous swinging bridges to welcome into the world any babies who did not wait for advantageous weather. These nurse-midwives worked on the theory that the nurses could go to the mother if the father could come for the nurses.

On December 29, Mrs. Breckinridge looked out the front windows of Big House at the scene in the valley below. Although the skies were still gray, the rain had stopped, but at the foot of the little mountain the Middle Fork was on a rampage. Riding horseback or by wagon to the railroad was clearly out of the question. Yet Mary knew she must make the trip down to Lexington. It was imperative. Her precious Juliette was pregnant, and her time had almost come. Certain possible complications made necessary her delivery in a hospital.

The director turned to a tall mountain man standing beside her. When she spoke, he sensed at once that her mind was made up.

"Mr. Taylor, we shall go by boat."

He rubbed his rough, unshaven chin. "That ol' river is a mite dangerous, ma'am."

She looked past him to where Juliette was moving silently about the kitchen. Usually the Swiss woman sang at her work, but for some days now she had not been her usual self.

Mary's chin came up. Her voice was determined. "It is more dangerous for us to stay here. Juliette can delay no longer, nor can those children who need medical care we cannot give them here. They shall go to Lexington even if I have to carry them."

The man broke into a slow smile. "I reckon that won't be necessary, ma'am," he drawled. "I just thought I'd better warn you."

She lifted her head proudly. "Danger and I are not unacquainted," she informed him. "We shall make the journey."

Early the next morning the little cortege filed down the hill from Big House to the river. They did not have far to go, for the water had risen almost to the front gate. Taylor Morgan stood at the bow of the *Ambulance,* as he had named the clumsy, flat-bottomed boat which was reinforced at the seams with pitch.

"You first, children," Mrs. Breckinridge said, marshaling two little girls aged three and six into the boat.

She took the next place and put a motherly arm about Joe, the frail eleven-year-old who, next to Juliette, was her chief concern. Ever since he had been brought to Wendover with an advanced heart condition, the boy had won all their hearts with his courtly old-fashioned manners and thoughtfulness. His home had been a poor mountain cabin, and his father was in a Federal penitentiary. The child was too weak and sick to be excited over the journey, but Mrs. Breckinridge had said he should go, and for him that was enough.

When everything was ready, Taylor Morgan cast off, and they were on their perilous way. The boat bobbed up and down like a cork at times, but their pilot held fast to his course. The three children took the voyage matter-of-factly, for high water was only a part of mountain life to them. It was as natural as the sun, the winds and the weather. If the adults were alarmed, they hid it well from the younger members of the group.

Although their destination was only sixteen miles away, their progress was slow. Twice Morgan guided the boat to shore. From there the passengers proceeded on foot while he took the craft alone through boiling rapids.

Finally at the creek known as Trace, the passengers landed again. Their pilot dragged the boat up on high ground and went off to locate a mule team. They had left Wendover at eight o'clock in the morning, and it was now five in the afternoon. Darkness lay all about them. The way to the railroad was across four miles of flooded trails. It was eight o'clock by the time they finally arrived in a wagon at the Krypton railroad stop.

When the great eye of the train's engine came rushing at them through the night, Joe, who had hardly spoken a word since they set out, seized Mary Breckinridge by the hand.

"Won't it get us?" he gasped.

She gently reassured him. Although he had endured a hard cruel life all his eleven years, it had not inured him to this new and terrifying experience.

They boarded the train, and Mary Breckinridge saw the children bedded down for the night. Then she sank into a seat beside Juliette, who seemed to be standing the trip very well.

"It's one thing to step out of one century into another," Mary told her with a smile. "It's quite another to be responsible for one's good friend and three sick children."

127

10 The Hospital at Hyden

The journey which had begun by boat did not end well. Joe did not respond to treatment at the Children's Hospital in Louisville. He died in "the settlemints," faraway from the mountains, leaving a loving memory in the hearts of all who knew him.

Going on to New York for speaking engagements, Mary was forced to undergo an operation which she had been postponing for a long time. While she was recovering at St. Lukes Hospital, she received the news that Juliette had died eight days after giving birth to a baby girl who had survived. They had named the baby Mary Breckinridge. The fact of Juliette's death, coming at the time it did, proved almost too much for the director.

Homecoming in April without Juliette to welcome her was a sad affair for Mrs. Breckinridge. Her friend's husband and daughter had gone back to St. Louis. Mary saw her little namesake only once before Juliette's married sister took her to rear as her own.

At Wendover the Morgan family had taken the place of the Carnis. There were Jahugh and Belle Morgan with their two youngest children and their niece Lulu. While no one could ever fill the vacancy left by Juliette, Mary and Belle Morgan soon became fast friends.

Mrs. Morgan's green thumb proved good medicine for Mary in her weakened, apathetic state. It had been a long time since the untiring director had used any time for her personal interests. Now she could not carry on her work with the nursing service because she was physically unable to spend long hours in the saddle. Nevertheless, lying in a hammock, she could direct Belle's gardening while Jahugh with his hoe and fork good-naturedly allowed himself to be managed by both women. Mary's father oversaw his workers not only in terracing the blossom paths (the mountain phrase for flower gardens), but also in laying out vegetable gardens in levels as he had seen them in Switzerland and the Austrian Tyrol.

Gradually the rest and the mountain air did their work. Although Mary was not yet ready to assume her old duties, she knew the time would not be long until she could do so. Meanwhile she knew also that winter was coming again and that there would be many weeks when Wendover, like other mountain places, must be self-sufficient. Last year she had been so involved in the work of the nursing service that she had hardly noticed Juliette's preparations for the colder months. But this year was different. She watched Mrs. Morgan as the latter canned beans and corn. She smelled the sweet odor of jam made from native mountain blackberries. She ordered a small house built where apples and potatoes could be stored. She wrote an uncle in Woodford County to get his recipe for smoking hams. Day by day, as naturally as the earth turns, she absorbed the healing sunlight and mountain air. Autumn found her whole again. She threw herself once more into the work of the Frontier Nursing Service, and because she was Mary Breckinridge, began one of the most ambitious projects of her entire career.

From the beginning she had known there must be a hospital. No matter how capable a well-trained nurse-midwife is, there are at times emergencies which require the services of a physician along with hospitalization. After having experienced a few such emergencies, Mary directed her energies toward plans for building a small hospital and procuring the services of a medical director for the Hyden area.

First a building site was donated. Following this, she set about the business of spreading the word of the great need for a hospital. Soon the drive for building funds was in full swing. Along with money, important gifts began to arrive. Mule teams for hauling, stone, lumber and free labor were as necessary as money.

For a whole year, while Mary was raising the money to start erection of the hospital, stone masons had been quarrying rock and hauling it to the site— Thousandsticks Mountain—overlooking Hyden.

"We had no choice," Mary told her critics, when they objected to the inaccessibility of the plant. "The valley is damp. The mists rise up sooner from the mountain. Up there we are well away from outdoor privies that could contaminate our wells. Then when exuberant young men ride into town on a Saturday night, shooting their pistols in the air, the patients will hardly hear the noise." Her eyes twinkled. "I really haven't come to the main reason. Every square foot of even semi-level land is already occupied."

Building a complex such as a hospital far from facilities generally taken for granted, such as water, light and sewage disposal, presented problems that often seemed to be unsolvable. What promised to be an adequate supply of water proved to be entirely inadequate for the hospital. The digging of wells was expensive, but a second well had to be dug. This new well produced salt water and was abandoned. Wells three and four were also failures.

Mary Breckinridge decided to approach this problem from a completely different angle. Her engineering advisers were convinced that water was there if they just knew where to sink wells. She called in a dowser, or 'water witch', a person who claimed to locate subterranean water by means of a willow switch in his hands which bends toward the ground at the proper spot.

Call it coincidence, call it luck. A new location was chosen for sinking a well. A new driller began to start the work. He drilled until he reached an underground river. Eureka! At last there was water aplenty for the hospital.

Slides are natural hazards for any building on the side of a mountain. After much experimentation, damage from this frustrating problem was brought under control. The water and sewage systems were also satisfactorily completed. Electricity other than that generated by Kohler engines was not available for six years after the hospital was constructed. Those machines furnished enough power for lights, sterilization and refrigeration, but the use of X-ray machines had to be delayed.

Down in the Bluegrass one of Mary's acquaintances with no firsthand knowledge of the mountains roused her ire when he displayed an outsider's ignorance about the situation.

"A builder's dream!" he sighed. "Stone masons at forty cents an hour, common laborers at twenty cents and carpenters somewhere in between. I wish I could find men at such prices in Lexington."

"You don't know what you are talking about," Mary Breckinridge told him indignantly. "Few men in the mountains have ever seen plaster. Certainly they know nothing about applying it. They have hardly heard of central heating. Electricity and plumbing are modern miracles in their eyes. Now do you think you would like to build the hospital at Hyden?"

"No," he said in an awed tone. "A thousand times no!"

In spite of everything the hospital rose slowly to completion. By the middle of 1928, it was finished and ready for occupants. It would house twelve patients as well as the district and the regular hospital nurses. Some years later the great verandas that ran the full length of the two floors on one wing were enclosed and heated. That change meant eighteen beds, eight bassinets and more clinic space; but it was 1949 before they could provide quarters for the nurses in another building. Moving the nurses meant a hospital with twenty-five beds and eight bassinets.

Hyden, Wendover and the nursing outposts had been in a state of happy expectation for days. It was now June, 1928. Preparations for the dedication of the new hospital extended much farther than the borders of Leslie County. In fact, they extended all the way across the Atlantic to Edinburgh. The executive committee of the Frontier Nursing Service had invited Sir Leslie MacKenzie and his wife to be present for the occasion, and they had accepted.

Mary Breckinridge looked forward eagerly to seeing her two old friends. She had received the inspiration for the Frontier Nursing Service from the Scottish Highlands and Islands Service founded by Sir Leslie MacKenzie. It was only fitting therefore that no other Highlander than Sir Leslie himself should dedicate the hospital.

Meanwhile she planned with her committee for the reception and entertainment of the fifty or more people who would be coming in to Hazard by train for the occasion. The rest of the way they would travel by horseback and mule team. At first Mary thought the matter of transport was well in hand with Marvin Breckinridge, the young daughter of John and Isabella Breckinridge, in full charge, and with Brooke Alexander to assist her. But these plans went awry. At the last moment Marvin was unexpectedly called home, and Brooke came down with a case of measles.

"I'll ask Martha Prewitt to do the job," Mrs. Breckinridge decided. "One can always depend on Martha."

Martha Prewitt was now Martha Breckinridge, having married Mary's younger brother Clif in Washington, D. C., a few months earlier. She had returned to Kentucky to be there for the dedication of the new hospital. Now at her sister-in-law's urgent request she took charge of transport, with some thirty horses and several wagons to be delivered at Hazard for the accommodation of the guests on the day before the celebration.

With that phase of the preparations assigned, Mrs. Breckinridge turned her attention to hospitality. She knew that about a thousand local citizens would be present for luncheon; indeed, almost that many persons seemed to be assisting in preparing or serving it. All seemed to be going well in that direction.

Now Mary Breckinridge went down to the Bluegrass. There would be a festive welcome for the MacKenzies in both Lexington and Louisville, and she had no intention of missing it. Entering into the spirit of the occasion, she did her best to give them a royal welcome. Then she returned to the mountains to be there to greet them upon their arrival.

Since neither nurses nor patients would occupy

the hospital until after its dedication, all the rooms and wards were available for the use of the guests. A number of Hyden families had offered their spare bedrooms, too. The big question seemed to be that of receiving the guests, especially Sir Leslie and his wife, who had come so far to be present for the dedication.

The director determined that she and some of her nurses would ride out on the trail to meet the incoming visitors. She hoped that the June day would not be too hot.

It was far from hot. On the day before, the skies opened, and blinding, torrential rains came down with a vengeance. A half hundred guests riding in special Pullman cars furnished by Mr. E. S. Jouett, vice-president of the Louisville and Nashville Railroad and also a trustee of the Frontier Nursing Service, had reached Hazard early in the morning, where breakfast was waiting for them at a hotel. After their meal, having marshaled her transportation forces, Martha Breckinridge started with the party for Hyden.

Not even the pouring rain had dampened the director's spirits. As soon as possible she and a group of co-workers started on horseback to meet the approaching cortege. They had gone about two thirds of the way when they met the incoming party, wet but undaunted, with Martha at their head. Horseback riders led the way, but Mrs. Breckinridge knew that the wagons and the buckboard which had been provided for the MacKenzies could not be far away.

When she met the first wagon, she found it completely covered by a tarpaulin.

"Is this the luggage?" she asked the driver.

He grinned from ear to ear. "No, ma'am. It's the band."

With that the tarpaulin seemed to rise of its own accord. Underneath it Mary spied a jumble of men and musical instruments, apparently none the worse for having rocked and jolted over the rough road.

"Pull down the tarp and keep dry," Mary urged, trying to keep the laughter out of her voice.

Soon she met the buckboard and the other wagons. They held a happy carefree crowd. Sir Leslie was on the front seat of the buckboard beside the driver. Behind them sat Lady MacKenzie and Mrs. Thruston Morton, chairman of the national committee.

The dripping tree limbs overhead could not quench the spirits of the travelers. One would not have believed that Mary Breckinridge had left them in the Bluegrass only a few days before. For a few minutes Kentucky and Scottish greetings mingled on the mountain road to Hyden as though the individuals concerned were meeting for the first time in many years. Then Mary Breckinridge turned her horse's head, and the procession advanced once more through the mud and the mire.

Not even fording the flooded Middle Fork shook the good humor of the passengers in the buckboard nor that of the people in the wagons which followed, although everyone was soaked through and through by the time the journey came to an end at Hyden.

Upon arrival the guests dressed in whatever dry clothing could be assembled. To say the least, they looked unusual when they came together in the dining room of the new hospital that night. They had already forgotten the discomforts of the journey and were wearing such apparel as the hospital could supply. Perhaps Dr. McCormick, the state health officer, wrapped in a sheet with all the dignity of a Roman senator, furnished the most entertainment for the crowd. The rooms were filled with talk and laughter. Someone coming in from outside reported that the stars were shining as though it had never rained.

The next day dawned bright and clear. Although the high water cut down the number of people who came for the ceremonies, at least five hundred were present from the surrounding countryside.

When the time came for the actual dedication, the guests assembled on the veranda which overlooked the small town in the valley below. Above them the Stars and Stripes and the Union Jack waved side by side. Mary felt a deep sense of thankfulness in her heart that representatives from Kentucky and Scotland could be together to launch the affairs of the mountain hospital. She felt also a marked sense of pride in her mountain people as they conducted the ceremonies.

The Leslie County judge presided, and the president of Berea College gave the invocation. Judge Lew Lewis, one of Mary's particular friends, gave the address of welcome. The members of the Perry County band, who had made the journey under the sheltering tarpaulin, played their instruments with a gusto which the rain had not lessened.

Lady MacKenzie was called upon to say a few words, as were Dr. McCormick and Mr. Jouett, whose help and generosity to the Frontier Nursing Service were known and appreciated.

At last the moment came when Sir Leslie Mac-Kenzie was introduced. Mrs. Breckinridge was deeply moved as she saw the tall, rugged man with the well-molded features and the Mark Twain moustache walk across the platform. She owed so much to his kindness and patience and most of all to the example of the magnificent organization he had headed in Scotland—the service which had been the prototype of the Frontier Nursing Service.

He began by comparing the Highlands and Islands Medical Service in his own country with the one in the Kentucky mountains:

> This hospital is the radiating center of the nursing service in these mountains. The maxim of the trained nurse is "You need me? I am ready." The hospital is a temple of service where the lamp never goes out.

In his final words, an act of dedication, he concluded:

> In all reverence, I dedicate this hospital to the service of this mountain people. The act of dedi-

cation will have the consequences beyond all imagination. It will evoke responses along the many hundreds of miles of these mountain frontiers and among the millions of their people. The beacon lighted here today will find an answering flame wherever human hearts are touched with the same divine pity. Far in the future, men and women, generation after generation, will arise to bless the name of the Frontier Nursing Service.

After his closing remarks and the luncheon which followed, Mary and her father took Sir Leslie and Lady MacKenzie home with them to Wendover for a few days of rest before they started on their long journey back. As usual, Wendover was full and running over. A crippled child was on a sleeping porch outside the double guest room occupied by the MacKenzies. A mother with her new baby was in the clinic. Motherless twins were among the patients. A nurse slept in the little post office where she could hear both the twins and the mother with her baby.

"It isn't very restful," Mary apologized. "For your sakes, I wish it were quieter."

Lady MacKenzie gave an understanding smile. "We wouldn't want it any other way. We are sharing Wendover with you just as it is, and we count that a high privilege. You have something very unique here, my dear."

When the MacKenzies departed in the buckboard, Mary on Teddy Bear accompanied them a part of the way. All three people felt a sense of sadness when the moment for parting came. None of them was young. Each knew that they might never meet again. Finally the last good-byes were said, and the buckboard rolled on. Mary sat looking after it as the horses went down the trail.

As the travelers went around the bend, something prompted Sir Leslie to rise and look backward. There was impressed upon his memory a sight he never forgot—the image of a gallant woman on a magnificent animal outlined against a forest back-drop.

11 The Frontier Nursing Service Grows Up

During the first five years of the Frontier Nursing Service—when Wendover became a beacon in the Kentucky mountains, the Hyden Hospital arose on the heights of Thousandsticks and the outposts sprang up one by one—of course the individual cases increased in number. However, to Mary Breckinridge and her helpers, a person was never a statistic. The human element stood out.

Invariably her staff shared her philosophy. One could hardly be with the director and not catch the contagion of her spirit. As the outposts increased, more cases came to the hospital. By now—the latter part of 1928—the hospital had a medical director. He was Dr. Hiram C. Capps of Tennessee with a residency in obstetrics. The state board of health had appointed Dr. Capps as public health officer in Hyden. This move left only part of his salary to be paid by the Frontier Nursing Service, for which the organization was duly grateful. Since Dr. Capps was not a surgeon, emergency work was done by Dr. R. L. Collins at Hazard. He thought little of covering the miles between in order to save a life. As Sir Leslie MacKenzie had said long ago, Mary Breckinridge had a way with her. The hospital had a superintendent, too. The director had brought Ann P. MacKinnon (Mac) in from the Beech Fork Nursing Center to fill that need.

Patients who came to Wendover and to the hospital at Hyden were like patients in any other hospital. They were there for appendectomies, tonsillectomies, childbirth and a variety of other needs. Then there were home gunshot wounds, hookworm cases, eye diseases and other ailments that were endemic.

It was not uncommon for little girls to be brought in badly burned from getting too close to an open fire. Their skirts blazed quickly if they were not careful. Their brothers clad in heavy overalls were more fortunate. More than once there were as many as six cases of burns from open fires in the hospital at the same time. When the number of burned cases soared near the thousand mark, the nurses began a campaign to dress the little girls in jeans like their brothers.

One day a father rode to Wendover with his fifteen-year-old daughter sitting on the horse behind him. The two were driving a cow ahead of them, and each carried a baby.

"My wife died with child-bed fever when the babies were two weeks old," the father explained to the nurses. "We have done everything we know for these little fellows, but it doesn't seem to do them any good. I'm a-feared they're like to die if you can't save them."

"Well, let's see what we can do," the nurse answered.

She was almost afraid the babies would draw their last breath before she could get their wasted little bodies into the waiting cribs.

"I'll leave my oldest 'un here with you so she can learn to take care of them properlike," he offered.

The nurse shook her head. "There is no need for her to stay yet. It will be some time before we can send the babies home. When we get them to eating and sleeping and growing, we'll send for her. That will be plenty of time."

Satisfied that their precious twins were left in kind and loving hands, the father and daughter returned home. The cow was left at Wendover in partial payment for the care of the babies. It was indeed some time before Enos and Eva left the sheltering care of the Frontier Nursing Service. Their stay at Wendover and the Hyden Hospital lasted a year. When they finally went home, they were in fine health. They were able to stand alone and showed six fine teeth with each engaging smile.

Soon Manny and Nanny came to take their places in the cribs. Their mother also had had child-bed fever. Although she survived, she could not nurse her babies and had found nothing that agreed with the tiny infants. At five months they weighed less than seven pounds each.

When at last they were sent home in good shape, they were followed by Moss and Ross. There seemed to be an unending stream of babies.

Because there was never enough good rich milk at hand or any good milk-producing cows, Mary Breckinridge put an item to that effect in the *Quar-*

terly Bulletin of the Frontier Nursing Service. Mr. B. H. Kroger of Cincinnati saw it. He quickly had a fine Holstein cow sent to Wendover. The animal gave six gallons of milk a day, which was more than the output of all the other cows put together.

In 1929 the citizens of Flat Creek asked Mrs. Breckinridge to provide them with a nursing center. After inspecting the neighborhood she was ready to act. The money was given by two Louisvillians in memory of their mother. Soon after their generous gift the local committee was organized and the land surveyed where the creek flows into Red Bird River.

Again Peacock and Tex were sent to oversee construction and open up the district. Installed in a three-room cabin for the time being, they were so impressed by its comparative spaciousness that they called it Buckingham Palace (in spite of the fact that it was located on Hog Wallow Branch).

From the first they were involved in nursing, public health and midwifery. In addition, several children broke out with scarlet fever next door to a maternity case. One nurse was forced to take the midwifery cases and the other handled everything else. At last the Caroline Butler Atwood Memorial Nursing Center, the fourth outpost, was in operation.

By the summer of 1930, the locations for two more centers had been decided upon, one on Bullskin Creek, the other at Bowlingtown.

Once more Peacock and Tex reported for building duty. They moved into a house on Leatherwood

Creek. It was painted white. They called their temporary residence the White House. No longer did they begin their additional tasks with fear and trembling. They had been responsible for the building of three centers so no time was lost in organizing their local committees and moving on through the preliminary stages. They even made an innovation in their own planning. One took the responsibility for the building of one of the new centers and one the other. Each could then use the other as consultant. By the end of 1930, six outposts were in operation.

With two nurse-midwives stationed in each, an area of approximately seven hundred square miles of horseback riding came under their supervision. Now the farthest patient was no more than six miles from professional care, and the centers were no more than twelve miles apart.

The centers splayed from the hospital and Wendover like fingers on the hand. They were built along the natural arteries of travel in the area—the Middle Fork of the Kentucky River, the Red Bird River and their tributaries.

A housekeeper-maid was a necessary member of the team in each outpost center. When the nurses arrived home after a long day in and out of the saddle, they fed and groomed their horses. Then they went into homes that were comfortable and ready for them. In winter a good warm meal and an open fire were eagerly anticipated. The many duties which every homemaker has to attend to were taken care of by these competent helpers.

In evaluating the first seven years of the Frontier Service, Mary Breckinridge experienced a sharp thrill of pride along with a deep feeling of gratitude. So many projects that at times had appeared to be almost impossible were completed and running smoothly. Now that matters had passed the formative stage, many wonderful things were beckoning. There would be setbacks. There had always been and there would always be. This she knew. But with the support of her excellent staff and the capable committees both within and beyond the mountains, the outlook was good.

The Hyden Hospital and the six outpost nursing centers were operating together and separately, according to plan. Specialists from Louisville and Lexington acted as consultants and gave their services free. Surgical, medical and dental clinics had been started.

Dr. Robert Sory of the United States Public Health Service, together with his nurse, had held the first trachoma clinic in 1927. In 1929 he held clinics in Hyden, Confluence and Big Creek. As a result of his pioneering work, a United States Public Health Hospital was opened at Richmond, Kentucky. Trachoma was the dread eye disease that ran rampant through the Kentucky mountains in earlier days. In 1950 the hospital closed its doors. There was no need for it, for trachoma was now a thing of the past in this area.

Worm infestation was another curse of frontier

people, especially children. Helminthologists held their first clinic in 1930. After the first clinic was over, it was apparent that until sanitation was thoroughly understood and practiced, these clinics must be in yearly session. It was difficult for the mountain people to believe in something which they could neither see, taste nor smell. They could not see intestinal parasites on a ripe tomato or a tempting rosy apple.

By this time an important branch of the Frontier Nursing Service was the section known as the courier service. There were both junior and senior couriers, all volunteers. The juniors, who had to be at least eighteen years old, came for periods of six to eight weeks each year. If they chose to return the second season, they were ranked as senior couriers and could remain for as long as they wished.

When a mountain man says he's going to take care of "the property," he means to feed the livestock—cows, horses, hogs and chickens. Before the couriers entered active service, they were thoroughly trained to take care of their "property," which during the early years of operation, meant the care of horses and mules. Needless to say, couriers were and are expert horsewomen. Later when jeeps became available and practical, the couriers cared for both animals and motors.

The couriers did not stop with routine duties. Once when a young courier from Chicago accompanied a nurse-midwife, she spent twenty-four of the busiest hours of her life in a one-room cabin. While the nurse tended her patient, the courier found every minute of her time filled.

The cabin was one of the poorest in the district. Snow blew in through a hole in the roof. A turned-over lard can served as a chair. As the courier moved about bringing wood in for the open fire, keeping the water hot and preparing meals, she frequently bumped her head on a side of salt pork that was swinging from the ceiling. All the while she worked under the careful scrutiny of a brood hen nesting in one corner.

The couriers were often daughters of Mary Breck-inridge's friends. As the word spread about the opportunity of serving with the couriers at the Frontier Nursing Service, a waiting list of names began to grow. During the winter, Bennington College students often took their practical field service at Wendover. More than two hundred couriers served the Frontier Nursing Service during its first twenty-five years. From the list of couriers, as time went on, came many trustees of the organization.

Mary Breckinridge on her horse Teddy Bear was crossing Middle Creek after a heavy rain. Suddenly a cry for help rang out over the water. She drew rein and listened. Again she heard the desperate cry. Quickly she turned her horse and rode through the swift water in the direction of the voices.

Two small children were standing huddled together in midstream on a rapidly disappearing island. In trying to cross the stream to get to their grandmother's house, they had been trapped by the rushing current. The water was already well over their ankles. In a short time they would have been swept downstream to destruction. Mary bent down from her saddle to take first one child and then the other to safety.

These were the motherless children of a woman who had died recently from another scourge of the Kentucky mountains—tuberculosis. Knowing nothing of health practices necessary in the stricken member's family, no separate beds, dishes and sputum cups had been used. These children and their father had suffered massive exposure to the terrible disease.

Mrs. Breckinridge discovered that the father too had tuberculosis. When he ran afoul of the law and was given a penitentiary sentence some weeks later, she wrote to the warden describing his condition and asking that he receive treatment. But it was not to be. When the time came for the man to pay his debt to society, he ran away.

Mary sent the two small girls to a preventorium in a neighboring state and resigned herself to the fact that the father would soon be in the advanced stages of the disease. Three years later to her surprise the man turned up in excellent health. He had come back to serve out his sentence. Upon questioning him, she learned that he had joined the army under an assumed name and been sent to the Philippines. Here when his condition became apparent, he was hospitalized and given the best care available until he recovered. Some years after this he died from an acute case of gunshot.

Soon after the children were rescued from the raging waters of Middle Fork, Mary suffered a tragic loss. Her horse Teddy Bear was turned out to pasture for a greatly needed rest. Always inclined to be venturesome, he climbed up a high cliff, slipped and fell. He dropped twenty feet and was wedged between a rock and a tree. It took four men to bring him out of his precarious position. His owner nursed her prized mount with loving care, but the injuries were fatal, and about a week later Teddy Bear died. Never again did Mary Breckinridge find a horse to take his place in her heart.

Following the stock-market crash of 1929 came the great drought of 1930. The poor farmland in the mountains could barely furnish sustenance for the older people and one or two sons. Yet with mills in the cities slowed down or closed, many of the men who had gone to work in the cities of Ohio returned to their old homes, bringing their families with them. Now the Frontier Nursing Service really girded itself for action. It faced a fight with disease which was aided and abetted by poverty and famine.

At the end of the summer of 1930, Mrs. Breckinridge went to Washington, D. C., to the American Red Cross. She took with her the results of a survey of available food in the mountain area for man and beast. This survey indicated that by January almost one fourth of the residents would be entirely without food, by March more than half and by June, 70 percent would be in the same condition. Later in the summer of 1931, by harvest time, 90 percent would be starving.

In January, 1931, the American Red Cross took over. They found the prediction that Mary had made to be true. One fifth of the population was being fed by the one eighth that had enough to share. These proud and independent natives took care of their own until the Red Cross could step in.

Mary Breckinridge and her staff never relaxed their efforts. She made an appeal over WHAS, the radio station of the *Courier-Journal,* asking for cows or canned milk for starving babies. As a result of her plea, the Frontier Nursing Service was able to give milk and cod-liver oil to thousands of the very young who would have starved without it.

In early April of 1931, the rains came. The drought was broken. Rejoicing echoed through the hills. Rafts were soon floating down the river with the current. Timber was again on its way to market. It was not raining rain to the mountain people. It was raining life and work. They could begin to live again.

On January 15, 1931, *The Forgotten Frontier* made its premier in New York City. Filmed toward the end of the silent motion picture era by Marvin

Breckinridge (later Mrs. Jefferson Wright, National Chairman of the Frontier Nursing Service), it proved a great success.

Mrs. Breckinridge's niece had been a courier with the service. She was so fired with enthusiasm for the cause that when she returned East, she took lessons in professional photography. Then she returned to the Kentucky mountains not once but several times in order to film the work of the nurse-midwives at all seasons.

The five reels portrayed life as it was lived in another century—life as she saw it in the mountains as a courier. It was necessarily life in the raw. In addition to shooting incidents and logging pictures, she secured many on-the-spot shots of Frontier Service nurses in action. Marvin Breckinridge knew what she wanted and always managed to be in the right spot at the right time to film it. Perhaps some of her aunt's mantle had fallen upon her shoulders.

The premiere showing, a benefit performance, proved more than worthwhile. But Mary Breckinridge wasted no time in stopping to enjoy it. By this time another idea was simmering in her brain.

She would undoubtedly have been a four-star general—a bishop—a prince of finance—had she been a man. She knew how to direct, to lead, to plan and to carry out those plans.

By now, 1932, she realized that more money was needed to counteract the effects of the drought. Less money than usual was coming in. Because this was the period of the Great Depression, gifts from friends of the nursing service were being cut down.

As Mary Breckinridge herself expressed it, "We decided to see what we could do with a cruise."

The Frontier Nursing Service worked out an arrangement with the International Mercantile Marine whereby they were allowed to sell tickets on the *M. V. Britannic* for a West Indies cruise in February and March of 1932. The Frontier Nursing Service was to receive 25 percent of every ticket sold. The projected cruise was on the way to being a success when in late 1931 disaster struck.

12 The Accident

It was November 29, 1931. Mrs. Breckinridge was on her way to the railroad accompanied by Dorothy Clark, a junior courier, and a boy who would take their horses back to Wendover. The director and the girl would make the trip East together. Mary Breckinridge had a full schedule of speaking engagements, and Dorothy was returning home to New York.

Mrs. Breckinridge was riding Traveller, a recent gift from the staff of the Frontier Nursing Service. In the two years since Teddy Bear's death she had ridden several horses, but had never claimed one for her own. Traveller was a product of the Bluegrass, a beautiful animal with strains of a saddle horse and a thoroughbred. He was a nervous mount with a tender mouth, and his mistress handled him with care.

It was raining, and Mary wore the service raincoat similar to that of the Royal Canadian Mounted Police. It was a practical garment with a roomy cape that protected the wearer from rain and snow. She had never worn it before when she was on Traveller.

"I shall be glad to get on the train," Mary told Dorothy. "There is so much to do in preparation for the West Indian cruise. I feel as though time is breathing down my neck."

The riders had reached the river and reined in

their horses to drink. Just as Traveller lowered his head, a puff of wind blew Mrs. Breckinridge's cape wide open. The frightened horse gave a tremendous leap. His rider, being an expert horsewoman, gave him his head. She would let him run up the trail beside Hurricane Creek and work off some of his terrific energy.

Almost at once she realized that he was out of control. He was galloping with fearful speed. A sheer wall of rock rose to her right. On her left a precipice dropped down to the creek. The raincape was still flapping in the wind and frightening Traveller more. Mary had no way of ridding herself of the garment. Meanwhile the horse sailed along as though he had wings. Mary gripped his sides with her knees, but she knew that neither she nor the horse could endure this pace for long. Time seemed to stand still.

She realized that the horse could probably outlast her, and she began to consider the best way to fall. There was not much choice. If she fell to the left, she would be a broken wreck at the bottom of the precipice. If she went over his head, he would trample her.

As Traveller sped on, she threw herself forward, dropped the reins and rolled to the right. The ground seemed to come up to meet her. The impact of the fall was a shock, but she did not lose consciousness. She knew she had been in sight of several cabins at the head of the hollow when she fell. Now to her ears came the sound of running feet.

"Why, it's Mrs. Breckinridge!" she heard a man's voice say.

With difficulty she opened her eyes. Several men were looking down at her with deep concern. A short distance away stood Traveller, no longer frightened by the cape. He was quivering from head to foot and blowing hard.

"Don't lift me," Mary begged. "I think it's my back. Wait for Dot Clark. She will show you how to move me."

The director lay without moving or showing by her expression the extreme pain which she was enduring. She had seen men such as those about her meet pain with a stoicism she found hard to summon now, but she knew she must do it.

It seemed an eternity before Dot came galloping up and leaped from her horse. She instantly took charge and sent the men running to cut down slender young saplings which they soon converted into poles. Then she showed them how to improvise a stretcher by turning their coats inside out and running the poles through the sleeves. This she slipped under the director inch by inch while her patient bit her under lip until she could taste the blood.

Even then Mary Breckinridge managed to open her eyes and give a wan little smile. "You're as good a nurse as you are a courier," she told the girl feebly.

The little procession started for the highway which led to Hyden. The men proceeded with extreme care, for their every movement made Mrs. Breckinridge wince with pain.

"She's a-punishin' a heap, but you'd never know it," one of the men said under his breath.

All her senses sharpened by pain, Mrs. Breckinridge heard every word they said. Dorothy Clark walking along beside her slipped a hand into hers. The woman on the stretcher never knew with what a viselike grip she held onto the courier's hand all the way to the paved road.

When they reached the highway at last, they found a car and loaded Mary Breckinridge into the back. With her feet resting on the floor, she reclined at a forty-five degree angle. Her head was level with the rear window.

"I'm trussed up like an Indian on a travois," she announced faintly.

The young courier smiled through her tears. Apparently nothing could destroy the spirit of this indomitable woman.

The bad news traveled ahead. By the time they reached the end of the highway, Dr. Capps from the Hyden Hospital was there to meet them. Under his direction the stretcher bearers took her up to the hospital on the little mountain. She hardly knew when she reached that haven, although she heard the doctor say to Ann MacKinnon, "Give her a fourth of morphine." With a feeling that she was in trained hands at last she let herself sink into a blessed mist of oblivion.

Travel on the jerky local train was out of the question, but she must be taken to Lexington where specialists could examine her. As yet there was no ambulance anywhere near Hyden. The nearest thing to it was an old-fashioned hearse at Hazard. During a hurried consultation, Mrs. Breckinridge heard someone suggest that vehicle.

"Bring it along," she ordered, her sharp ears overhearing the whispered controversy. "I suspect I'll be the first living human to ride in a hearse. I'll even let Mac share the honors with me—and I shall need my secretary Wilma, too."

All the hospital staff that could be spared gathered to see her depart. As the boxlike black vehicle disappeared around the bend, the disconsolate group turned one by one and prepared to go back to work.

"It's just awful," sobbed a new young nurse. "She may never come back."

Tex swept her a withering look. "Want to bet?" she asked in a voice that failed to hide her emotion. "It will take more than a fall from a horse and a ride in a hearse to finish *her*. She'll be back. Just wait and see."

The orthopedic surgeon at Hazard made X rays before the trip to the Bluegrass. When Mary learned that the pictures would go with her, a plan began to form in her mind. At Berea she directed her secretary to call the Lafayette Hotel in Lexington for rooms.

"But, Mrs. Breckinridge, you must go to the hospital," said Ann MacKinnon, aghast.

"Nonsense, Mac," her patient replied. "There is no better orthopedist anywhere than our Dr. Hagan at Hazard. Dr. Marmaduke Brown will be willing to accept his X rays. I have a mountain of work before me which I can do better in a hotel than in a hospital. If I once get there, the doctors will not be likely to move me. Call for rooms, Wilma."

Dr. Brown and Dr. Josephine Hunt, Mary's cousin, met the little cortege at the Lafayette Hotel. After Mrs. Breckinridge was made comfortable in her quarters, Dr. Brown studied the X-ray pictures for several minutes. Then he walked to a front window and stared at the Main Street traffic below.

"You may as well tell me," Mary said.

His usually gruff voice was noticeably gentle. "Your back is broken—a crushed second-lumbar vertebra. You know what that means."

"Just what I thought," she answered matter-of-factly. She might have been discussing a third person with the surgeon. "In plain words, a broken back. But I can't stay here, forever, Duke. We have a West Indian cruise to finance. I have speaking engagements I can't break. You must fix me up so I can leave here as soon as possible."

Dr. Brown regarded her gravely. "You will need at least eight weeks on a Bradford frame, and then we will fit you with a metal brace. It will be months before you can travel."

With that he turned and walked out of the room. After he had gone, Mary Breckinridge lay in stunned silence for an hour or so. This could not be happening to her. It seemed like a bad dream. But it was happening, and it was time she faced the situation squarely. Someone else would have to carry on while she was incapacitated. But first there was one person who must know what had happened.

Ann and Wilma jumped as her firm voice rang out into the room. "You will find a little brown address book in my purse. Cable Adeline in England. Tell her I need her prayers," she said simply.

Through the years she had written or received a letter from the anchoress every few months. Every member of the Frontier Nursing Service staff in the mountains had a secondhand acquaintance through their director with Sister Adeline of York.

Before dinner that night Wilma reported that the cable was winging its way across the Atlantic. Her patient received the news with a smile.

"Mac, you and Josie Hunt go down to dinner," she ordered with something of her old manner. "Wilma will stay with me. She can have something sent up or go down to the dining room later."

In an hour Mac and Dr. Hunt returned to the room. Wilma, her finger at her lips, met them at the door.

"Asleep?" Dr. Hunt said in surprise. "I thought she would be wide awake and in considerable pain. Dr. Brown left her a sedative."

"She dropped off in less time than you would believe," Wilma reported. "She has been sleeping like a baby ever since. Her anxieties and worries seemed to fade away after I told her the cable was on the way."

Josephine Hunt bent over and took her cousin's wrist gently in her hand. A moment later she straightened up. "Pulse perfectly normal," she announced. "Condition generally good." Her lips parted in a smile. " 'There are more things in heaven and earth than are dreamed of in your philosophy, O Horatio,' " she finished.

That evening Mrs. Breckinridge received a reassuring cable from Sister Adeline in which she expressed her sympathy and promised her prayers. The next morning, news of her accident having traveled fast to all metropolitan centers where there were Frontier Nursing Service Committees, offers of aid and help began pouring in.

After Mary had been placed in the Bradford frame and had become somewhat adjusted to it, her thoughts turned toward the mountains.

"Duke, is there any reason I shouldn't go back to Hyden?" she asked the doctor. "I could stay in our own hospital where Dr. Capps would be close at hand. Dr. Hagan is in Hazard. I will have capable care and yet be close enough to base to keep up with what is going on."

Dr. Brown grinned. He had known Mary Breckinridge for many years. "It might be better for all of us, including you, if I allow you to go back. You worry and fret too much when the miles lie between you and your nurses. Just be sure to return here sometime late in January to be fitted with a steel brace."

Before she left for Hyden, Mary had a visit from Mr. Charles Manning, who had been treasurer of the Frontier Nursing Service since its beginning. He had already sent out a letter, he said, to all subscribers. He had asked each of them to contribute to a fund which would take care of the service's financial affairs and relieve the director's mind while she was recovering. He, along with the national chairman, Mrs. S. Thruston Ballard, and Dr. A. J. A. Alexander's widow, were subscribing five thousand dollars to get the fund started. The patients under the Frontier Nursing Service would not suffer.

Soon Mary Breckinridge was on her way to Hyden. This time she traveled in a Lexington ambulance. Upon her arrival at the mountain hospital she found Christmas preparations in full swing. Mary settled down at once in her hospital bed to join in the Christmas planning and also to reduce the stack of correspondence that by now had assumed gigantic proportions.

One matter that needed her attention was the retraining of the horse Traveller. She asked the advice of several expert horsemen as to whether he was an "outlaw." She received a negative answer from each. He was merely a highly sensitive thoroughbred startled by her raincape.

In England the practice of having a goat around a thoroughbred stable had been started when it was observed that the small animal had a quieting effect on the high-strung horses. A goat was brought to the stable to be with Traveller. Mary soon heard that he had accepted his new companion, and the two were becoming fast friends. Definitely the retraining of Traveller was on the way.

Another problem to which the director needed to turn her attention was the selection of a new medical director for the hospital. Dr. Capps had decided to do postgraduate work and then go into private practice. Dr. John H. Kooser was chosen to replace him. He would remain at Hyden for eleven years until he volunteered in 1943 for the Medical Corps of the United States Army.

On Christmas Day, 1931, the entire staff of the little hospital joined in making it a pleasant one for their director. The tone of the day was set when she opened her eyes in the morning to see a new plaque hanging on the wall beside her bed. A gift from Mac, it read: "JUST ABOUT THE TIME YOU THINK YOU CAN MAKE BOTH ENDS MEET, SOME-ONE MOVES THE ENDS." With a hearty chuckle, Mary turned on her pillow, hearing the morning sounds as the hospital began to stir and a new day dawned.

13 The Years Go By

When the *Britannic* sailed for the West Indies in February, 1932, there was a passenger in a new steel brace aboard. Mary Breckinridge had been invited as a guest by one of her cousins. Not to be outdone, the International Mercantile Marine invited Mary Willeford (Tex) to go along so that Mrs. Breckinridge would have a nurse with her.

The cruise proved delightful and memorable. The Frontier Nursing Service cleared only six thousand dollars, but the executive committee decided to try another Caribbean cruise for the spring of 1933. This one, however, proved a financial failure, for the United States was still in the throes of the Great Depression and conditions had not improved. This latter effort marked the end of ventures in cruise projects by the Frontier Nursing Service.

Mary Breckinridge slowly recovered from her spinal injury, and the work of the hospital and the centers went on. Her father died in December, 1932, at the age of eighty-six. The ties between father and daughter had been close, and she missed him greatly. During the six years he had lived at Wendover, he had identified with the people his daughter served, and they mourned him as though he had been one of their own.

Although Mary returned to the mountains in

April, 1932, after the *Britannic* cruise, it was April, 1933, before her doctors permitted her to resume horseback riding.

When that day came, she lost no time in making a tour of the outpost centers. Although spring rains caused floods and forced her to make several detours, she persisted in making the journey. It proved a triumphal one with a royal welcome everywhere she stopped. Residents in the area and workers in the service uttered a little prayer of thanksgiving for her return. Literally and figuratively at last Mary Breckinridge was back in the saddle again.

The Frontier Nursing Service, along with the rest of the nation, was still in the dark days of the depression. Subscriptions from every corner of the country had dropped in size, although in most cases they were lowered rather than discontinued. Mrs. Breckinridge was forced to cut the staff. This placed the brunt of the work on those who remained.

In spite of that move, the esprit de corps of the service remained high. When liabilities in the form of bills and notes due piled up, the executive committee informed all nurses and secretaries that payment of their salaries was possible only on a two-thirds basis. There were those among the workers who felt that for financial reasons they must leave. Others who were able to accept the cut stayed on and formed a truly dedicated personnel.

Serving under Mary Breckinridge was always an exciting experience. She never allowed the organization to stand still. The American Association of

Nurse-Midwives, organized in 1928, was started in Kentucky and incorporated under the laws of the commonwealth the following year. Its original members, numbering sixteen, were all on the staff of the Frontier Nursing Service and at that time comprised the only nurse-midwives in the United States.

During the early years of the Frontier Nursing Service, Julia C. Stimson, head of the nurse corps, visited the mountains of Kentucky. After a tour of Mary Breckinridge's territory, she paid the nurses a high tribute. In an article in the *Quarterly Bulletin* she said:

> If out in the world one met a nurse who could deliver babies, superintend primitive carpenter work and well-digging, dose and care for horses, advise about farming, teach untrained girls cooking, live cheerfully by candlelight and with enamel basin and pitcher bathing facilities, keep well and full of humor and common sense, one would think the combination of all these qualities was worthy of comment. And down there in that Nursing Service seventeen or eighteen nurses were doing all these things—and each one thought her particular center and her particular work and her particular patients were the very best.

When Mary Breckinridge came back to Wendover in 1932, the American Association of Nurse-Midwives was on a firm foundation and increasing in usefulness and service every year. The nurses received their training in Great Britain, since the first postgraduate school in midwifery was not opened on the American continent until that year. To Mrs. Breckinridge's joy its first supervisor was a nurse who earlier had been in the Frontier Nursing Service and had been sent by them to England for midwifery training.

As time went on, Mary realized that the cost of sending American nurses to England for midwifery training was more than a depression-depleted budget would bear. Some day she planned that there would be a school for midwives right in the center of the Frontier Nursing School territory. Meanwhile she would keep on using her powers of persuasion to induce British nurse-midwives to cross the Atlantic and come to the mountains of Kentucky.

In 1939 the entry of Great Britain into World War II brought about indirectly the realization of that dream. Now it was a necessity to establish a Frontier Graduate School of Midwifery. Eleven British midwives at Hyden and Wendover asked to be released from their duties at the earliest possible moment so that they might return to service in their homeland. That would mean the depletion of the staff. Until the war was over, the director could hope for no more recruits from Great Britain. Nor could she expect, with England at war, to send nurses there for midwifery training.

Accordingly the director quickly set the wheels in motion. The state board of health agreed to give the examinations—oral, written and practical—at the end of the training period, after which the newly organized Frontier Nursing School of Midwifery would grant diplomas. Then and only then would these graduates become Certified Midwives (C.M.) licensed to practice in Kentucky.

The curriculum for the first School of Midwifery was patterned on the six-month course for graduate nurses in Great Britain. It included classroom instruction, lectures, field work among expectant mothers and the delivery of twenty normal cases.

By fall of 1940 the eleven British midwives who had asked to be released were back in England. As the war progressed, so did the nurse shortage in the mountains of Kentucky. Times such as these, filled with emergencies and tensions, brought to quick notice a person's capabilities. Such a situation existed when the Frontier Nursing School of Midwifery was started. Its first dean became Dorothy F. Buck (Bucket) who served until her death in 1949.

Since sufficient staff was not available in the early 1940's, double duty became a necessity. The head nurse-midwife in the Hyden Hospital now became a teacher as well. Helen E. Browne, who had served at an outpost first, held the first position and now assumed the second one also.

Mrs. Breckinridge, who like Miss Browne had trained at Woolwich, found in her one of the most brilliant teachers she had ever known. Her ability to communicate with her students was outstanding.

Both these women possessed the rare combination of being able both to serve and to supervise.

In spite of shortages in staff and material the work of the service went on, for babies kept coming during times of war as well as during periods of peace. And so did disasters.

At Marblehead, Massachusetts, on January 9, 1942, Mrs. Breckinridge received a telegram from Wendover. It said:

> Garden House burned completely yesterday afternoon. All at lunch. Cause unknown. No one hurt. Two full tanks kept fire from spreading. Lucile's main books saved and major contents. Safe found in good condition today. Everything else lost. Frightfully sorry. Have written Marblehead. Fire completely under control. Tanks refilling. Everyone carrying on.

The cause of the fire that consumed Garden House, the location of the executive offices and some sleeping quarters was never known. It occurred about 12:30 P.M. on January 8, 1942. The flames were first seen by two men passing along the road.

Their shouts of "Fire! Garden House on fire!" rang out through the cold clear air. Inside Big House the staff members deserted their meals in record time. Some rushed to man the emergency hose, while others ran to the close-by stables to lead out the horses.

169

The hose worked perfectly, but the fire had gained too much headway. It ate its way steadily through the large log building. As the flames borne by the wind leaped upward and also toward the barn, a second hose was turned on that building. Fortunately the wind did not carry the flames with enough force to ignite the barn, but while the outcome was still uncertain junior couriers led the horses to safety.

From Marblehead, Mrs. Breckinridge dispatched a letter to Wendover. Putting the loss of the valuable records out of her mind, she asked her co-workers to set to work at once on plans for a new Garden House. In this request she had a twofold purpose. Not only was she eager to have the building replaced, but she knew the task would keep the minds of the staff off their losses.

Meanwhile as the word spread over the nation that Wendover had suffered the loss of an important building, gifts of money began to pour in to cover the cost of rebuilding. Checks ranged in size from small amounts to several thousand dollars. With no appeal whatever from the Frontier Nursing Service, the gifts continued to flow in. They came freely from people everywhere who had heard of the incredible Mary Breckinridge and her great work.

Soon the new Garden House took shape. It was rebuilt and refurnished. Larger and better equipped than the old one, it again housed offices on the first floor and bedrooms on the second. The old and new staff members joined in donating funds for the Wendover dispensary—a memorial to General

James Carson Breckinridge, Mary's brother who had died a few months earlier. He had once visited at Wendover and won the hearts of the nurse-midwives by saying that they were the only other people in the world besides the Marines whom he had found ready to go anywhere when a sudden call for help came. Mary was deeply touched by the consideration and thoughtfulness of her nurses in giving the memorial, and from their act she garnered strength to go on with her duties.

It was in 1951 that Mary Breckinridge made a temporary change in the pattern of her life. She spent more than a year in writing the story of the service which is inseparable from the story of her life. She called her autobiography *Wide Neighborhoods*. The trustees of the Frontier Nursing Service, eager to have a record of this great philanthropic endeavor and its founder, raised more than $55,000 to finance the organization while its director took the necessary time for its writing. Before the book was published, the author conveyed all rights in it to the Frontier Nursing Service. All royalties were to go direct to that organization.

The publication date was timely. It marked the end of the service's first twenty-five years. The author was glad to have the opportunity of sitting down and taking stock, collecting loose ends of information, and reviewing the unbroken years of loyalty on the part of the organization's friends and supporters.

By now she had spent the greater part of the money left her by her mother. Most of it had gone into building Wendover and financing its operation during the first five years. Her partial records show that during that time she entertained 328 guests. More than half of these were patients. She had made welcome all who came to Wendover for 2,184 days. All this proved an expensive undertaking.

It was not until 1930, when the Frontier Nursing Service could assume the upkeep and running of the place, that she deeded Wendover to them. On the advice of her lawyer she reserved a sum of her capital sufficient to enable her to enter an old ladies' home, should she live to an advanced age and find it necessary. That bit of her property she left intact. The rest she used from time to time for the project nearest her heart—the Frontier Nursing Service. Her money did not run out until 1938. At that time she agreed to take a salary like the rest of the workers. (The highest salary at that time, except for the one paid the medical director of Hyden Hospital, was $125 a month.)

During the twenty-five years that she had been at Wendover, many changes had come about. Jeeps had joined horses—and as time passed, would replace them—as a means of transportation. Telephones were installed in most nursing centers. Refrigeration had come to the outposts as early as 1941 through the efforts of a board member who discovered that those centers had no ice. (The first refrigerators were serviced by motors operated by kerosine lamps.)

The Frontier Nursing Service was no longer linked to any degree with another century. It was rapidly becoming a part of the twentieth century in many areas, although devoted and dedicated nurses still answered mothers' pleas for help up in the hills and down in the hollows.

Mary Breckinridge was growing older—she was seventy now—but she had never ceased to care about the needs of the present and to look ahead to needs of children and their mothers in the future. She could hear in her heart her father's gentle voice saying, "Live simply and love deeply." Those two things she did. And deep within her was the undimmed memory of Breckie, whose untimely death had set in motion the wheels of the Frontier Nursing Service, which was now the center of her life.

Another decade passed. The director was nearing eighty. Another of her dreams was beginning to materialize. For many years she had longed for a chapel at the Hyden Hospital. Back in 1940, her cousin, Dr. Preston Satterwhite of New York City, had presented her with a beautiful fifteenth-century stained-glass window depicting St. Christopher and the Christ Child.

She had determined that this window, which had hung for many years on a stairway at the Satterwhite home, would one day be the focal point of a greatly desired chapel adjacent to the hospital on Thousandsticks Mountain.

Every year at Christmastime she told an expectant audience at Wendover and also at Hyden the legend of the ferryman Offerus, who had gone out on a black and stormy night to carry across the raging river a small child who seemed to grow heavier and heavier and almost caused him to be swept to destruction before they gained the other side. Upon delivering his burden safely, Offerus found to his amazement that he had born no other than Jesus Christ and all the sins of the world. Thenceforth the ferryman became known as Christ-Offerus, or St. Christopher, the Christ-Bearer.

Telling the legend had become a part of Christmas in the little mountain community. And Mary herself was sure that one day the precious stained-glass window would be housed in a chapel worthy of it.

Dr. W. B. Rogers Beasley, who succeeded Dr. Kooser as the director of Hyden Hospital, evolved a plan of action. Knowing how greatly Mrs. Breckinridge longed for the chapel, he conceived the idea of having each of the 12,000 babies delivered by the Frontier Nursing Service donate one dollar to the cause. The plan was set in motion and money, along with other gifts and pledges, began to come in.

As the months passed, the Christopher Chapel began to rise. When it was finished, the little stone building was an architectural gem. Mary Breckinridge could hardly believe that her dream had come true. But it had—even to the words expressing the aim for which it was being built:

That it would be used by all who wished in the Frontier Nursing Service territory and Hyden Hospital area—Baptists, Presbyterians, Holiness, Church of God, Church of Christ, Episcopalians—all who wished to ask God's blessing on their illness, or on their work, to offer thanks for those delivered in childbirth, for those recovered, for those departed, here would find a proper and convenient place.

14 The Great Days

It was February 16, 1961. This was the eightieth birthday of Mrs. Mary Breckinridge, director of the Frontier Nursing Service. Wendover had been preparing for the celebration for weeks. An eightieth birthday, her co-workers thought, was a special event that needed a special observance.

The day promised to be fair and warm. When Mary Breckinridge first awoke, she thought she heard music. Listening intently, she realized it came from high on the mountain behind Big House, and that it was the resident nurse-midwife at Wendover playing her cornet. When the hymn selected for that morning ended, it was followed by "Happy Birthday to You." Mrs. Breckinridge, now thoroughly wide-awake, smiled with delight. If this was what was meant by a second childhood, it was a most enjoyable state of being. In spite of the years that crowned her, she was happy with a youthful zest.

"And why not?" she thought gratefully. "They all are treating me as though I were a queen, bless their hearts. Katherine Carson here from Knoxville, Margaret Preston Johnston up from Lexington and every nurse who can be spared in the area is about to descend on Wendover for my birthday dinner. Truly I am a fortunate woman."

Shortly before noon the clan gathered—her very own clan, the workers of the Frontier Nursing Service—plus friends and relatives from far and near. Even Dr. Beasley, director of the Hyden Hospital, had managed to be present. In all, some sixty persons sat down together at noon.

Before they began the meal, Dr. Beasley, after a few preliminary remarks, raised his glass and said: "A Toast to our teacher, to our friend, to the Rose of Wendover!"

There was tumultuous applause as he sat down. All eyes were focused on the recipient of the toast who looked with loving eyes upon the assembled guests. It was a poignant moment. Although Big House was filled with the sound of voices and laughter, there was also an undercurrent of sadness, for all the people assembled and Mary Breckinridge herself knew that this was an occasion that came only once in a lifetime.

But there was no time for even the hint of tears, for Wendover was in a gala mood. After the guests had served themselves from the buffet repast at the long dogtrot table decorated in festive birthday trappings, they sat down in the spacious living room at smaller tables.

The guest of honor had ordered her favorite menu —spoonbread, turkey hash, turnip greens and spring onions—and judging from the number of guests who returned to the table for second helpings, they thoroughly approved her choices.

The pièce de résistance arrived toward the end of

the main meal when an employee brought in an enormous round birthday cake topped with eighty red candles. The size necessary to supply so many guests had puzzled the culinary department until Alabam Morgan, cook at Wendover for many years, had suggested baking the cake in a dishpan.

Blazing with lights, the enormous confection had been set down in front of Mary Breckinridge, whose blue eyes gleamed at the sight. She blew away at the candles until every gleam was extinguished. Then with a steady hand she removed the tapers and carefully cut the first piece of cake.

"Just as my father did it in this room when *he* was eighty," she exulted. "Only today I have someone as old as I am to share it with me."

She smiled at Mrs. Becky Jane Morgan, who was sitting nearby. Mrs. Morgan, the oldest Frontier Nursing Service employee, was also the only other octogenarian at the dinner.

Mrs. Breckinridge handed the cake knife to another Wendover nurse. Cutting sixty pieces of cake was no small job, and she wanted to enjoy her dessert with the other guests.

When dinner came to an end, the tables were cleared away, and the company gathered about the great stone fireplace in the west wall of the living room. Everyone present knew that it was a replica of the one at The Brackens, the home of her girlhood in Canada. On this February day more than sixty years later, the crackling flames on the hearth lightened the hearts of the spectators and brightened the farthest corner of Big House from the hand-hewn beams in the ceiling to the well-stocked bookshelves on the inner wall.

Conversation spiced with reminiscences about the early days of the Frontier Nursing Service flowed steadily all afternoon. The hours passed quickly, for there was never a lull or a letdown in their gay spirits. Altogether it was a memorable time which passed all too quickly, but it was etched forever on the minds and hearts of the participants.

More than a year had passed since Mary Breckinridge's birthday dinner at Big House. Now another long-awaited Great Day had arrived. Not even the director's eightieth birthday had called for such a widespread celebration. That had been more or less a personal affair, while this day of September 22, 1962, had been heralded far and wide. Sometimes it seemed to the staff at Wendover as though everyone all the way to Great Britain and beyond knew all about Mary Breckinridge Day. Certainly there were those in Africa, Asia, the Philippines and other far reaches of the globe—nurse-midwives who had begun their work and in some cases received their training in the mountains of Kentucky—keenly aware of all the events scheduled to take place in the little town of Hyden. A constant stream of congratulatory cards and letters bore their writers' loving greetings to Mrs. Breckinridge and gave ample notice of their feelings about her.

This day was not intended to be a private occasion. It was the coronation scene, so to speak, of their leader, and everyone concerned was determined that it should be a never-to-be forgotten affair. Planned by the Leslie County Development Association, it marked a time to honor a great lady in their midst, for Mary Breckinridge was now well into her eighty-first year.

Saturday dawned fair and clear. The surrounding hills were beginning to be touched with shades of red and gold although summer still lingered. Townsfolk were barely beginning to stir when arrivals began coming into Hyden. Mountain people are by habit early risers, and this particular day seemed to call for something a little extra.

The lodestone which was drawing all traffic was the county high school, a flat modern building spreading out on a hill across the bridge from the state road. Young and old, the travelers came on foot, on horseback or muleback, in wagons, and because this was the twentieth century in cars both old and new.

Suddenly an expectant air fluttered through the waiting people. All heads were turned in the direction from which came the music of a not-too-distant band.

"Here they come!" someone shouted.

Across the bridge all traffic had been halted over on the state road. Eager spectators in the schoolyard craned their necks and peered in that direction. The parade had started with an escort of state police leading the way.

First came Betty Lester, in uniform of course, on her white horse Kimo. Next were the twenty-one units that made up the major part of the procession. For a town of fewer than 400, they were an impressive sight.

There were floats from all the outpost centers, and from Hyden Hospital, Wendover and Dry Hill. Bands from Clay County and Hazard High School did their part, and fresh young voices from the high-school glee club rang out in the morning air. The Frontier Nursing Service jeeps from surrounding centers were filled with nurses in their gray-blue uniforms. The hospital station wagon filled with nurses lent its presence to the occasion. There were still more floats representing other organizations in the area. At the rear of the procession were automobiles and mule-drawn wagons holding mountain people who, like the individuals on the floats and in the cars, were there for one purpose only—to honor Mary Breckinridge.

As the parade made its way toward the playing field behind the schoolhouse, all eyes turned in the same direction. High up on a hill sat a figure on horseback. Mary Breckinridge, eighty-one years young, in the gray-blue uniform of the Frontier Nursing Service, was reviewing her troops.

Hampered by the cruel steel brace and unable to ride horseback for any length of time, she was nevertheless mounted this morning on Doc, also a veteran of the Frontier Nursing Service, to receive the tribute that three and even four generations of mountain people were extending her. Her head held high in the sunlight, she viewed the passing line like the general that she was.

Finally the last of the procession disappeared from her view. It was bound for the playing field behind the school. Now accompanied by her guard of honor of nurses and couriers, Mary Breckinridge rode down to join the others.

The Beech Fork float had been designed as a speakers' platform. One half of it formed a rostrum. The other half was occupied by a log cabin. In its open doorway Mrs. Breckinridge sat down to view the program.

One main speaker of the day was Dr. Francis Massie of Lexington, who through the years had worked closely with the woman being honored today. The other speaker was Dr. John Kooser, former medical director of Hyden Hospital.

The third speaker proved a distinct surprise, especially to Mrs. Breckinridge. A little blond eight-year-old girl, standing on a stool to reach the microphone, announced that she had been the ten thousandth Frontier Nursing Service baby to be brought into the world.

The last person to speak to the assembled people was Mary Breckinridge herself. In a voice that trembled slightly she told her listeners that she thanked them and loved them. Few among her listeners were unmoved, and even a few old rugged mountaineers in the crowd dabbed furtively at their eyes with bandannas.

Finally the program ended with the singing of "My Old Kentucky Home" by the high-school glee club. The crowd began to scatter for lunch. Many families had brought picnic baskets, and the out-of-town guests were invited to a meal prepared for them in the schoolhouse.

The Great Day was over. Due honor had been given, and Mary Breckinridge had received homage from a loving and grateful people. She felt with a thankful heart that her cup was running over.

Mrs. Mary Breckinridge died on May 16, 1965, three weeks before the forty-first annual meeting of the trustees and members of the Frontier Nursing Service in Lexington on June 8. She had seen forty years of service with the organization to which she had given the major part of her adult life.

Epilogue

Under the leadership of Mrs. Breckinridge the service, which had begun as a tiny plant on May 28, 1925, in Frankfort, Kentucky, had grown, in her words, to be a mighty banyan tree, "yielding shade and fruit to wide neighborhoods of men."

In the forty years during which Mary Breckinridge served the Frontier Nursing Service, there were 57,640 registered patients. Of these 24,809 were babies and toddlers, 9,698 schoolchildren and 23,133 adults. They gave 248,191 inoculations. There were 27,903 patients admitted into Hyden Hospital, which was opened in the fiscal year 1928–29. In all the forty years there were only eleven maternal deaths of which nine were puerperal and two cardiac.

The Frontier Nursing Service, inspired by its parent organization in Great Britain and Scotland, has become international. Inseparable from it and still a part of it is the American Association of Nurse-Midwives organized at Wendover in 1928. Today the little group of sixteen has increased to more than 255. These women are scattered all over the world, serving in remote and isolated spots. All members in the United

States who find it possible to attend come to an annual meeting each year at Wendover. It is impossible to estimate how many lives of mothers and babies have been saved through the united efforts of these sister organizations.

Today Mary Breckinridge sleeps with her forebears in the lot of her paternal grandfather, John Cabell Breckinridge, in the Lexington cemetery. Breckie and Polly lie beside her. But in a sense she lives on through the Frontier Nursing Service, which is as active as ever in the mountains of eastern Kentucky.

Each night the lights of Wendover shine out over the Middle Fork of the Kentucky River in Leslie County. During the day—and frequently in the middle of the night—nurse-midwives still travel out over the territory from there and from the nursing centers. They travel now in jeeps rather than by horseback, but they are inspired by the same desire to serve that possessed their founder. "If the father can get to the nurse, the nurse can get to the mother," they say. And they mean it.

Those on the staff at Wendover who can possibly be there still gather at four o'clock each afternoon in the living room for tea as they did in Mrs. Breckinridge's day. Helen E. Browne is director—Mary Breckinridge planned it that way—and when she is not away on a speaking tour, she is present for the daily tea hour at Big House. As of old, the dogs of Wendover wander in and out the lovely old living room to receive their favorite tidbits from their mistresses.

Since a motor road was built from Hyden to Wendover, guests come from many countries: Australia, Austria, Belgium, Brazil, Burma, Canada, Ceylon, Chile, China, the Congo, Costa Rica, Denmark, Egypt, England, Ethiopia, Finland, France, Greece, India, Indonesia, Iran, Ireland, Japan, Laos, Lebanon, Malaya, Pakistan, Panama, Peru, Scotland, Sweden, Taiwan, Thailand, the Netherlands, the Philippines, Turkey, Vietnam.

The predominant number of guests is made up of physicians, nurses, midwives and social workers. These individuals come to get help with their problems of rural planning. They are eager to study the organization of the Frontier Nursing Service. They are desirous of learning about frontier techniques. Sometimes they bring ideas of value to the mountains of Kentucky. As it has been since its beginning, the Frontier Nursing Service is a beacon lighting not only the territory it serves, but also the distant countries which have heard of it.

There are warmth and graciousness at Big House still. Those who knew Mrs. Breckinridge will not forget her. Those who never knew her are conscious of an atmosphere which is unique, for Wendover forms the hub and center of the Frontier Nursing Service operations. There are the executive offices from which plans still go out for the immediate area and for far-flung places where workers trained in the Kentucky mountains go to render service. These are the graduates of the Frontier School of Midwifery. They are now serving in several American states, Canada, New Zealand, New Guinea, the Middle East and parts of Asia, Africa and South America. The essence of the labor of the first director lingers still.

In the words of a physician from India who once visited at Wendover: "She had in her the elegance of past ages, the gracious daily life, and the courage to ride a space-craft. . . . I shall cherish her memory."

But perhaps the inner core of her being which made her the woman she was is best expressed in the motto of the Frontier Nursing Service: "He shall gather the lambs with his arms and carry them in his bosom, and shall gently lead those that are with young."

At the forty-third annual meeting of the Frontier Nursing Service in Lexington, Kentucky, in 1967, an announcement was made to the effect that ground will be broken in Leslie County in the spring of 1968 for a new $1,600,- 000 hospital at Hyden in memory of Mrs. Mary Breckinridge.

The new hospital, which will replace the old one on Thousandsticks Mountain, will occupy two acres of level ground in the little mountain town. Instead of the present crowded hospital licensed to operate sixteen beds but sometimes accommodating twenty-five—"You can't turn away a patient," says Mrs. Breckinridge's successor—the new Mary Breckinridge Hospital will have fifty beds.

When the announcement was made of the forthcoming hospital, nearly half the $1,600,000 had been raised through advance pledges and donations. Meanwhile a new documentary movie is planned to be used in fund raising for the memorial to Mrs. Breckinridge. This time the premiere will be in Kentucky, and it will be used with a background of dulcimer music performed by native Kentuckians.

The Frontier Nursing Service has changed with the times. Horses have given way to jeeps. With the coming of roads in eastern Kentucky many mothers now come to the hospital to have their babies, although others still prefer their confinements at home. And now the somewhat inaccessible hospital on a mountain overlooking Hyden will give way to a more practical one on level ground. Some things have changed, but the will, the determination, the invincibility of Mary Breckinridge remain. In that sense, she lives on.

Bibliography

Breckinridge, Mary. WIDE NEIGHBORHOODS: A Story of the Frontier Nursing Service. Harper & Row, New York, 1952.

Gardner, Caroline. CLEVER COUNTRY: Kentucky Mountain Trails. Revell, New York, 1931.

Poole, Ernest. NURSES ON HORSEBACK. Macmillan, New York, 1932.

QUARTERLY BULLETIN of the Frontier Nursing Service, Volume 1, Number 1, June, 1925—Volume 41, Number 1, Summer, 1968.

Index

Index

INDEX